MY SILENT PRISON

MY SILENT PRISON

A CAUTIONARY TALE
OF SPOUSAL ABUSE
IN THE 1 PERCENT

NUNZIA MONDO

HOUNDSTOOTH
PRESS

COPYRIGHT © 2025 NUNZIA MONDO

All rights reserved. This publication contains the opinions and ideas of its author. It is intended to provide helpful and informative material on the subject addressed. It is sold with the understanding that the author is not engaged in rendering medical, health, safety, or other personal or professional advice or services. Readers should consult with their own medical, health, or other professional about their own situations or before adopting any ideas or suggestions in this book. In addition, mention of specific professionals or organizations in this book does not imply endorsement by the author, nor does it imply that such professionals or organizations have endorsed the author.

Names and identifying characteristics of some individuals have been changed, as have identifying details surrounding some events. Unless otherwise stated, dialogue has been re-created or adapted for space reasons.

Website addresses given in the book were accurate at the time it went to press, and the author is not responsible for changes to third-party websites.

MY SILENT PRISON
A Cautionary Tale of Spousal Abuse in the 1 Percent

FIRST EDITION

ISBN 978-1-5445-4699-5   *Hardcover*
      978-1-5445-4698-8   *Paperback*
      978-1-5445-4700-8   *Ebook*

This book is dedicated to

Michael Smerconish, who doggedly pursues the truth in an era of rampant and shameless lying;

Shireen Abu Akleh, Palestinian-American journalist murdered while doing her job;

The sacred memories of Munich's White Rose group, especially Christoph Probst, Hans Scholl, and Sophie Scholl, who had the courage to mount resistance against Nazi terror and lies, even unto death;

Former Detective Constable Maggie Oliver of the Greater Manchester Police Force, for her relentless fight against grooming gangs as well as the complicity of UK authorities who continue to cover up the travesty of organized child sexual abuse;

My parents, whom I didn't appreciate until it was too late; and

All victims of spousal and partner abuse, particularly the children.

CONTENTS

INTRODUCTION 9
1. VIGNETTES OF VIOLENCE 15
2. THE OFFICE 37
3. MISTREATMENT OF OUR CHILDREN 47
4. MANIC SUNDAY 59
5. HOW TO WIN FRIENDS AND INFLUENCE PEOPLE 69
6. DO SWEAT THE SMALL STUFF 77
7. CONTROL FREAKERY 85
8. GASLIGHTING 101
9. FAST DRIVING: AN ADDICTION AND A FORM OF ABUSE 109
10. DEFINITELY DISGUSTING 117
11. DESTROYING ME AS A WOMAN AND UNDERMINING MY POSITION AS MOTHER 127
12. THE FINAL THREE YEARS: HELL ON EARTH 153
   CONCLUSION 195
   ANNEX 203

INTRODUCTION

Well before Freud came up with psychoanalysis, he accessed his own unconscious by sitting down and writing for three days, a method of self-examination based on an influential essay penned in 1823 by Ludwig Börne, "How to Become an Original Writer in Three Days."

Freud's principal clients were the bored, frivolous upper-class Viennese ladies known as "the Hysterics." They spilled their secrets and dreams, free-associating on his green couch at Berggasse 19. As I type, it occurs to me that I could be their twenty-first-century counterpart. Nevertheless, I hope both you and my shrink will take me seriously.

Initially, this book was just for me—and writing it has taken far more than three days. I attacked the project in fits and starts but persisted in the vain hope that committing thirty-plus years of hell to paper would help me make sense of an adult life that started out with so much promise. My piecemeal efforts have gone some way toward helping me sort out, understand, grieve, forgive, and move on. But the scarring that I, a well-educated woman living a prosperous and comfortable life, received at the hands of a cruel, fickle, and abusive husband will never be totally healed.

As I delved into my own sordid story, I had to face the profound damage I had caused my children because of my determination to keep my marriage and family together. There are no words to express the sorrow and heartsickness I'll carry to my grave for subjecting them to such crippling dysfunction. I cannot adequately express the remorse I feel for not sticking to my guns the time I grabbed my toddlers and sleeping baby and fled the house almost three decades ago. Or later, when the kids were older and I left several times on my own, for always caving in to my ex-husband's entreaties to return—entreaties accompanied by promises to change, promises to seek help.

As my story revealed itself over the course of months and years, I also recognized my duty to provide personal insight into spousal abuse for the abused, or potentially abused, of any socioeconomic circumstance, race, gender, or sexual orientation. It's in this light that I confess a horrifying epiphany. It was only when I conducted this postmortem that I realized I'd gotten stuck in this quagmire partly because of my implicit and unexamined belief that spousal abuse didn't happen to the likes of us. It was my delusion—no, let's be honest, my prejudice—that intimate partner violence was the preserve of African Americans, Hispanics, and white trash, the final term itself a form of gross disrespect and abuse. No one is trash, and neither you nor I have the right to label another person with such demeaning language. Words can kill, and once you've fired them from your rocket launcher, there's no taking them back.

* * *

This is my story. It's true, but to protect the guilty as well as the innocent, I've changed identifying details of certain characters and events. However, the essence of each anecdote I recount remains, and many incidents went down exactly as described. Where necessary, I've been intentionally vague about sources of information. I've also thrown in the occasional red herring to put you off the scent. You won't figure out who I am; I promise, though, that you know a spouse or partner who's inhabiting a silent prison much like the one I belatedly escaped.

Herein, I'll regale you with incredible tales of my thirty-year relationship with my ex-husband, Tom. I refrain from analysis to the extent possible; nevertheless, it has sometimes been necessary for me to explain certain behaviors in mental health terms. I highlight the cycle of abuse *as I experienced it* against the backdrop of Tom's borderline personality disorder (BPD).[1] In 2021, Katherine Collison and Donald Lynam of Purdue University conducted a meta-analysis of 163 studies and found that BPD and antisocial personality disorder are "significantly and positively related" to perpetration of intimate partner violence.[2] From my vantage point, a detailed chronology and analysis of my own marriage suggests a powerful link between Tom's BPD and the abuse I endured.

However, it would be irresponsible and unjust of me to go beyond the scope of these findings and make any general claims about the correlation between personality disorders and spousal abuse. What *are* the root causes of spousal abuse? Experts have many different answers, from certain beliefs and ideologies around gender to the abuser's own childhood traumas. Indeed, each abuser has been subject to their own set of pernicious influences over a lifetime. My aim is to start a fruitful conversation among my readers on spousal abuse, which destroys individuals, families, and our social fabric.

My story, particularly its sequencing, has gone through several iterations. I hope my final version, which is presented thematically, not only provides optimal education and a bit of entertainment but also makes sense to victims; their friends, families, and colleagues;

---

1 BPD, along with narcissistic, histrionic, and antisocial personality disorders, falls into the classification of cluster B personality disorders as defined by the *Diagnostic and Statistical Manual of Mental Disorders (DSM-5)* of the American Psychiatric Association. Cluster B disorders are those in which sufferers have difficulty with impulse control and emotional regulation. Please see Annex for a list of the BPD traits and the boxes Tom checked.

2 Katherine L. Collison and Donald R. Lynam. "Disorders as Predictors of Intimate Partner Violence: A Meta-analysis," *Clinical Psychology Review* 88 (2021): 102047. https://doi.org/10.1016/j.cpr.2021.102047.

professionals in mental health and the justice system; and those of you who are simply interested in the subject of abuse.

Now that I've come to grips with how incredibly long my story is, I'm including only the most illuminating examples of the abusive behavior I experienced. The abused among my readers will clamor for more as they take a scant teaspoon of solace from learning they're not alone. Others of you will think I've become mired in detail, losing the forest for the trees. I've done my level best to present an accurate and complete picture, which, in my view, has necessitated confronting and fleshing out many unsavory moments from my relationship with my ex-husband. I hope I've struck a balance for all my intended audiences.

※ ※ ※

I end this introduction with some warnings and an appeal.

First of all, while the vast majority of cases of spousal abuse are women victimized by men, we shouldn't kid ourselves. Women also victimize men with cruel and mercurial behavior and sometimes physical violence. The particular tragedy of male victims is that when they finally lash out with an ill-considered slap across the face or a push—because, quite frankly, relentless abuse can make even the saintliest of us snap—they often end up in legal trouble, losing visitation with or custody of their kids and sometimes going to prison. We shouldn't forget about partner abuse in the LGBTQ community either. For a host of reasons, this is an issue that has long been swept under the carpet. In 2015, a review of forty-two studies by the Williams Institute at UCLA Law School concluded that the prevalence of intimate partner violence in nonheterosexual relationships is as high as, and possibly higher than, in heterosexual relationships, a finding confirmed by subsequent studies in both the US and the UK.[3]

---

[3] Taylor N. T. Brown and Jody L. Herman, "Intimate Partner Violence and Sexual Abuse among LGBT People," Williams Institute, November 2015, https://williamsinstitute.law.ucla.edu/publications/ipv-sex-abuse-lgbt-people/.

The fact is, *people* fall in love, lured by seeming adoration that sweeps them off their feet and, in the process, fall into the trap of disordered or unhappy souls who crave love but are incapable of true love and intimacy. Depending on the personalities and circumstances of both abuser and victim, their sick dance can last for decades—or a lifetime. Many victims hold out the hope that they'll finally reach their partners with logic. Unfortunately, abusers don't operate in the realm of logic. Indeed, logic is the abuser's worst enemy. A logical argument that calmly and constructively responds to what he just said or did isn't a reason to reconsider but, rather, a reason to escalate. Reason is a red rag to a bully.[4]

If you believe you're the victim of any of the categories of abuse I describe in this book, please conduct a brutally honest assessment of your relationship. If you conclude that abuse is an abiding feature of your marriage, you need to think seriously about extricating yourself. Take legal advice, consult mental health professionals, and ask for assistance from government agencies or other organizations qualified to help domestic abuse victims. If you do decide to exit, you will need to plan and execute carefully and quietly for your own sake and that of vulnerable family members. Think about it: your departure is likely to enrage your partner further. By the same token, remaining in the relationship in the hope that you can school him in the subject of abuse and help him reform is almost certainly a grand delusion that could subject you to more hell. Over time, you'll lose your self-esteem, your health, your sanity, and possibly even your life. Take off your rose-colored specs and trust yourself to know whether you need to leave for the life of peace and freedom you so deserve.

Finally, although I again admonish anyone involved with an abuser to consider leaving as soon as practically possible—*because he is exceedingly unlikely to change and you will not be spared*—we

---

4 For simplicity, I henceforth refer to abusers as male but with full recognition that it isn't always a "he" who perpetrates abuse. I have also reduced the term *spousal/partner abuse* to *spousal abuse*.

should remember abusers are people, too, and in many cases were themselves abused. While they shouldn't be let off the hook for their evil, entitled actions, civil society has the ethical imperative to design interventions for them. Abusers inflict untold damage, but many have suffered greatly, often in childhood, at the hands of people who were supposed to love and nurture them. How can we bring love and healing into their lives and, more importantly, stop the cycle from continuing in their children and stepchildren? Change is probably not achievable for some abusers. However, there is anecdotal evidence that some can be rehabilitated over time with dialectical behavior therapy (DBT), a version of cognitive behavioral therapy that trains abusers to identify, face, and actively change their reactions to the negative emotions that motivate their abusive behavior.[5]

I don't have all the answers. I'm still processing the reasons I landed in and persisted with my marriage and continue to ponder my own culpability. But I've had to start my healing journey somewhere. I wonder if any alarms will start to ring as you read the myriad accounts of verbal abuse and physical violence, little lies and massive deception, gaslighting and blaming, petty nastiness and gross disrespect, and neglect and adultery that came together to create an epic tragedy. I hope my story won't be yours.

---

[5] Lundy Bancroft, author and expert on domestic abuse, has designed a five-step program for the abuser who wants to turn his life around. DBT is the fourth step for the BPD abuser, available only when he's done the heavy lifting required by the first three stages, which include listening and accepting his partner's complaints, understanding his denial of abusive behavior, and ending retaliation. See https://lundybancroft.com.

CHAPTER 1

VIGNETTES OF VIOLENCE

A PEA-BRAINED CUNT

The "honeymoon" period of B-school romance was over, but I was too clueless about abuse and too head-over-heels to recognize what was happening. Our MBA class held an impromptu election for a student council to represent our interests with the administration. Ironically, our British business school didn't attend to the needs of its customers, namely us. Among our class were a number of Englishmen recently returned from New York, several North Americans, and a few thrusting Brits jolly sick of the socialist inertia Margaret Thatcher, only halfway through her tenure as prime minister, hadn't yet been able to eradicate. The student council was very much in the "get your skates on" Thatcherite spirit, and, accordingly, the election took place just days after the initial proposal.

My devoted and charming boyfriend of four months, Tom Mondo, ran for a place on the council. His campaign speech was specific, forceful, and rousing, and we were both sure he'd win a place. He lost, however, to the older and wiser fellows. He accepted defeat graciously, but by the time we got back to my flat, he was in a rage. I'd never seen a grown man react like this. In truth, I hadn't taken the election all that seriously. It was a spur-of-the-moment decision, and I suspected the council would be toothless anyway.

As I made tea, I told Tom I was just as mystified as he was about the result and tried in vain to comfort him with thoughts of other projects. He got angrier and angrier, like a small child having a temper tantrum. I was totally bemused: how could someone lose control over something so minor? I felt the need to change the mood, which I thought some lighthearted ribbing would achieve. That's what my family and friends would have done to me in the event of a sense-of-humor failure. Big mistake.

Tom perceived my attempt to make him laugh as mocking and he grew even wilder with fury. Without warning, I was knocked to the floor when his fist struck my mouth and nose. I'm not sure how many times I was punched as I lay there on the floor, but I clearly recall some choice words I'd never expected to hear. I was *a pea-brained cunt* and *a stupid bitch* who needed to *shut the fuck up*. In the brief moment it took Tom to assault me, he blackened my eye, caused my nose to swell, lacerated my gums and the inside of my mouth—and shook me to my very core.

Immediately full of remorse, Tom took me to the closest A&E (emergency room). While Tom admitted to staff what he'd done, the doctors treating me didn't ask if I wanted to file a police report. Maybe filing a police report wasn't standard procedure, or maybe they'd just seen too much of this to care. Whatever the case, I was released after a few hours, and we were left to get on with our lives, which in my case meant missing a week of classes until the bruising and swelling subsided.

I can already hear you asking why the hell I didn't break it off right then and there. The fact is that I'd never personally experienced or witnessed a verbal or physical attack by a man on a woman in my entire life—not with previous boyfriends, between my parents, within my extended family, or in my wider community. Remember: it didn't happen to the likes of us. And while I'd worked on a trading floor where I'd regularly heard high-decibel foul language as part of both celebratory and deeply pissed-off refrains, I'd never had a man say the C-word to me or even utter it in my presence.

On this occasion, the use of the C-word was more than a cultural difference between British and Americans. Tom's face was contorted with rage and his words were venomous, which was almost as stunning to me as his physical assault.

However, blinded as I was by this new love, I was quick to brush off the entire episode. *Of course, this was just a one-off; Tom was having a bad day. No reason to overreact or tell him to get lost.* I was wild about this thoughtful Englishman, especially the contrast his puppy-like devotion and generosity presented to the behavior of my former self-satisfied cheapskate boyfriend, who'd taken me for granted for so many years. I was absolutely soaking up the adulation and enjoying my perch atop the pedestal I'd been placed on by Tom, who said he felt ten feet tall when he walked around London with me. With this shocking incident, the first round of love-bombing, the kickoff to an ongoing cycle of abuse, was definitely over.

HOW DARE YOU GET YOUR WORK DONE!

Before going to London for my MBA, I'd been educated at a top US university and worked for an investment bank in New York. In neither of these environments was there any tolerance for sloppiness or lateness. I brought this work ethic with me to business school. When we were assigned vast quantities of papers in the mostly unfamiliar topics of corporate finance, organizational management, logistics, marketing, and business strategy, I got going pronto.

Therefore, after the breaking-in period of forging friendships and a romance, I allocated an hour and a half of our two-and-a-half-hour lunch breaks to working in the library. The very first time I attempted to carry out my plan, I was called on the carpet by Tom, who told me in no uncertain terms that this was rude and unsociable. I relented and stayed in the canteen, engaging in useless banter every lunchtime for a couple more weeks. I ultimately decided, though, that I really couldn't fritter away so many hours. I was able to strike a compromise with Tom that I'd be able go to the library directly after lunch a couple days a week and began slithering out of the canteen along with other serious members of the cohort. Even before the postelection attack I described above, Tom's abuse was presaged by the erosion of my freedom of action.

Apparently, I was also rude when I was unwilling to accompany the in-crowd for a few pints at a nearby pub with convenient opening times. I was able to put my foot down when it came to drinking at lunch. But I still faced the thorny issue of how to handle the 5:00 p.m. reopening, which precluded any serious work later in the evening, especially because pub sessions could easily end at closing time. (This particularly British ritual was made all the worse by the lack of food to absorb the massive quantity of alcohol being consumed.) I was a willing participant far too often, but thanks to my water-every-other-drink strategy, I was able to avoid the hangovers others suffered many a morning. (I'm sorry to report that our pub ringleader died from cirrhosis of the liver at the age of thirty-three.)

In the first term of the MBA program, we had to complete many short assignments, which I submitted on time and did fairly well on—much to the great surprise and chagrin of the Brits, who asked to borrow my marked papers to see what this dumb American had to offer. At the end of the first term, we were assigned five major papers, due after our monthlong Christmas holiday. I spent my break in Europe with friends who allowed me to work all day, as long as I emerged for lunch and supper.

When I got back to London for the start of the second term, I'd finished my coursework. Tom hadn't started his. Not a single assignment. Not even the reading or research for one. He had a complete meltdown as I unpacked my neatly arranged folders, all ready to be handed in. It's difficult to convey to someone who's never been with such a wack job what happened when I pulled this heartless and insensitive stunt.

It was bedlam. Tom was literally shaking with fury that I'd had the gall to finish my work. It was as though I'd committed a crime against him personally. After he completed the bulk of his meltdown, he demanded to read my papers and crafted his own, to a great extent, on my content. I was able to assuage his lingering anger by typing his papers for him. Dear Reader, it may be hard to believe, but this was the mid-1980s. Almost no one had a personal computer, but I had an electric typewriter and the impressive speed of fifty-nine words per minute.

Similar scenes were repeated throughout our MBA program when I'd fully prepared myself for other coursework, presentations, or exams. One night before an exam he hadn't bothered preparing for, Tom (who has an IQ a full ten points higher than mine) began to scream, flail his arms, and cry in panic, calling me a bitch and ordering me to teach him the material by the next morning. He wasn't angry with himself and wasn't begging for help. You see, because I'd done this awful thing—preparing for something we'd both known about—it was my responsibility to fix the problem I'd caused. Under the circumstances, I felt rather resentful and unsympathetic, but refusing to cooperate wasn't an option.

By this point, I'd recognized I was dealing with a man capable of any sort of violence, physical and/or verbal, if he didn't get what he wanted. Tom had made me feel responsible for him, and I'd bought into it. I knew that even admonishing him for his disorganization before acquiescing to his demands meant risking life and limb. As it was, I had to spend twenty minutes listening to his effing and blinding against me.⁶ After these soul-destroying and energy-sapping preliminaries were over, I could get down to the business of teaching Tom all he needed to know to ace the test.

THE BODY CHECK

If you don't count the intermittent slaps and pushes, the second physical assault happened a few months after the first one. It was March, almost dusk, on an icy, blustery Sunday afternoon. As we walked down Gloucester Road in South Kensington, looking for a church service to attend, I said something innocuous and silence-filling that irritated Tom.

I never learned exactly how I'd misspoken. I really must have rubbed Tom the wrong way, though, because he rammed his shoulder into my chest and his hip and elbow into my stomach as though he were an ice hockey player checking his opponent. I fell hard on my bottom and ended up sprawled on the frozen sidewalk. I was in severe pain and had difficulty standing. Tom yanked me up, discharging a few choice words as he did so.

Etched in my brain is the look on the face of the elderly lady who witnessed all this. She saw the assault, heard Tom's words, and appeared outraged but never said a thing.

Many years later, when I had an MRI for a back problem, the doctor asked when I'd broken my coccyx. I replied, "Never," and he said I most assuredly had and showed me the film to prove it. I have to wonder if it happened on that chilly spring afternoon because I can't recollect any other time I could have sustained such an injury.

Like the elderly lady, I'd uttered no words of protest. In fact, I kept the pain to myself and literally and figuratively kept on going. That was the problem. I was all about placating. If I did something wrong, Tom's reaction was extreme, causing me guilt and profound anxiety. If I misconstrued something, it was my fault, and

---

6 "Effing and blinding" means releasing a torrent of obscenities.

I needed to "clean my ears out and listen more carefully." If Tom misconstrued something, it was also my fault because I hadn't made myself clear.

I was the frog in the boiling water. Gradually, but over a relatively short span of time, I came to devote considerable emotional energy to peacekeeping, preempting problems, and scrambling to rectify them when I caused them. I was taking it all on myself, and the belief settled in that I was constantly making avoidable missteps, which I was then totally inept at fixing. I wasn't used to people whose impatience was a central and unapologetic aspect of their everyday behavior. I wasn't used to people who screamed and swore at the drop of a hat. I wasn't used to physical violence. I thought I must be provoking these extreme reactions. Bit by bit, I reached the conclusion that there might be something faulty in me.

WHY ARE YOU SUCH A BITCH?

After business school, I stayed in London to work for a former boss, running a pool of assets for a global insurance outfit he'd recently joined. I also had to oversee our substantial UK property portfolio, which included five luxury residences in Kensington and Knightsbridge. I was lucky enough to get one for myself, and the other four were at the disposal of visiting executives. About four months into my tenure, Tom's parents lost their home and needed a place to stay. He asked if they could borrow one our properties for a month. I said OK, but with the provisos that it was only a month and they paid for a full cleaning upon departure.

They moved in right away, with Tom often staying with them in the lap of luxury. They optimized their stay by housing visiting relatives from abroad and entertaining frequently. One evening, I was invited to dinner there to meet two Rhodesian businessmen Tom's parents were considering partnering with.

Afterward, Tom drove me back to my place and asked my opinion of the Rhodesians and their business proposition. I told him

I thought the idea sounded interesting. That was as far as I could go, though, because I hadn't seen the business plan and couldn't understand what their projections were based on. *Had they done any market research? More important, did they have access to financing?* My parents-in-law certainly didn't. (In addition to having their home repossessed and their credit cards canceled, they'd been declared bankrupt. Their long-suffering younger children had been thrown out of their boarding school for chronic non-payment of tuition.)

As a newly minted MBA, I could be expected to pose such questions. However, Tom wasn't interested in my business nous. He wanted to know my *impression* of these men. I confessed I found them a bit strange and insincere, a bit hard to pin down. I guess Tom was looking for a yes-woman because he was so desperate for his parents to finally succeed at something that he was willing to suspend his intelligence, top-notch training, and extremely suspicious nature. When I politely clarified my position on the men themselves, Tom became enraged. For fifteen minutes, he screamed without pause, "Why are you such a bitch? Why do you want my parents to fail? Why are you so negative?"

I was completely flummoxed. When someone asks you for your impression of another person, it's usually to confirm their own. Tom had asked for an honest opinion, and I'd given him mine. I was already in the habit of retracting words, so I immediately said I was sorry and willing to admit I was wrong. I added that it was precisely because I didn't want his parents to fail that I gave him my honest reaction to these guys.

All this clarifying, retracting, and apologizing was futile because Tom was already what I would later term "on a roll" and wouldn't listen. He just played the screaming, effing, blinding tape on a loop. When we reached my intersection, I felt incredible relief, but he wouldn't let me out of the car. Instead, he drove me around the block five times, vomiting out the same insults and ones I'd never heard before. I was scared, I was tired, I was in tears—and I was profoundly confused. I really thought I'd given Tom what he wanted. Finally, at the end of the fifth circuit, the traffic light did me the favor of turning red. I quickly unlocked the car door, jumped out, and ran to my apartment.

How did this end? I honestly can't remember when or how Tom and I moved on from this contretemps, although I do entertain the possibility that neither of us spoke of it again. We resumed the same sick rhythm of our relationship. Due to lack of funds, Tom's parents and the Rhodesians weren't able to continue their relationship. And in what was to become a pattern of entitlement and gross irresponsibility, my future parents-in-law overstayed their welcome by three weeks and never paid for a cleaning of the property.

I HAVE TO WORK IN THE MORNING, YOU FUCKING INCONSIDERATE BITCH

This anecdote will cause you to question my intelligence, my judgment, and even my honesty. I look back and wonder with a lump in my throat and tightness in my chest why this incident didn't make me run for the hills.

We were both about nine months into our new jobs. Tom, who was staying mainly with me at my South Kensington apartment, was out that evening with Pandora, an old friend of his from university. I wasn't worried about their continued connection but was concerned about the vast amounts they drank—sometimes five to six bottles of claret between them. I needed to have Alka-Seltzer on hand for Tom's return.

While Tom and Pandora were out wining and dining, I was at a nearby laundromat washing Tom's clothes and my bed linens because my new washer-dryer was inexplicably already on the blink. Somehow, within months, I'd been sucked into covering the entire roster of domestic duties for both of us: grocery shopping, cooking, washing dishes, picking up dry cleaning, and doing laundry. I knew Tom was likely to be home around 11:15 p.m. and would want to be in bed by 11:30 at the latest. When I realized it was already 11:10 and I still had two wet loads with no dryers available, I knew I was in trouble.

This was before the advent of cell phones (which you'll find out later didn't make my dealings with Tom any easier), so I went to a red phone box to call Tom at the apartment and explain my predicament. My intention had been to tell him how sorry I was and that he should go straight to bed. I would creep back in with the folded laundry as quietly as possible and sleep in the spare bedroom so that I wouldn't wake him.

Tom had, in fact, arrived home by the time I called, but I never got the chance to explain. His ranting and raving began right away, and he said he was coming to deal with me. I was terrified because I could hear in his voice how uncontrollably angry he was—and because he knew exactly where I was. Before I had a chance to hatch an escape plan, he'd already power walked his way to the laundromat. As I saw and heard him coming toward me, I began screaming and crying, pleading for help from the many people who were still out and about. Tom was so menacing that grown men dispersed. I ran into the corner grocery store, and Tom ran after me. As I darted down the aisles, I called to the store manager to please ring the police. He didn't want any trouble and demanded I leave the store.

Somehow, I made it out without Tom catching me. I then ran into the currency exchange place, where I'd spotted two burly guys standing at the counter. As Tom followed me in, screaming, swearing, and threatening me, I begged them for help. As wild as Tom was, the two of them could have easily subdued him. It was clear I was in danger, but they didn't come to my rescue. They dashed out, and Tom had me cornered.

Right then and there, in the currency exchange place, Tom unleashed in greater detail what a fucking inconsiderate bitch I was, knocked me to the floor with his first punch, and gave me a few more just to make sure I got the message. Even as I lay there, curled up in a ball, weeping in pain and fear, he continued to scream at me. Among the crowd gathered to watch the spectacle, no one came to my assistance.

After a few minutes, the enormity of what he'd done must have hit Tom because he called his father and sister, who arrived quickly. Tom's sister gave him quite the berating and brought me back to my place. Tom's father brought him home, wherever home for the Mondos was at that point. For some reason that I can't recall, I didn't go to the hospital. However, I did sustain a black eye and swollen nose that kept me out of work for a week.

Tom was incredibly regretful. Because I trusted him, I was receptive to his overtures, which included flowers, jewelry, sweet talk, and an effort to be patient and respectful. He didn't move back in with me, though. Instead, he began living with a mutual friend of ours.

CARPE DIEM—EXCEPT I DIDN'T

Later that spring, Tom broke up with me without much ado and in a cold, clinical way. I later discovered that this was because Tom had had his head turned by another woman. Tom had decided he could do better than me. I'd been *discarded*. I was mystified as well as upset: everything had been going so well, so why had I been dumped from one day to the next?

Let's take this moment to digress from *Vignettes of Violence* to talk through the cycle of abuse: the prelude of love-bombing, followed by devaluing, discarding, and hoovering. This and similar abuse terminology has been in widespread use for some time. As I belatedly became acquainted with the terminology and the conceptual framework of abuse it springs from, I embarked on my journey of understanding. What a gift to be able to make some sense of the excruciating bewilderment I'd experienced over three decades!

In recent years, I've also benefited enormously from the online resources provided by clinical psychologist Dr. Ramani Durvasula (known as Dr. Ramani), licensed professional counselor of mental health Todd Grande, and relationship coaches Christina of Common Ego and Stephanie Lyn.[7] In their unique and accessible styles, these four professionals have educated me on the subject of abuse and its typical progression and shown me that I'm not alone. Their respective areas of expertise have been the portals through which I've been able to form a retrospective of my life with Tom. Without their information and insights, I'm convinced I'd still be the tongue-tied, timorous, profoundly depressed shell of a divorced woman who blamed herself completely for her predicament. I give credit where credit is due and thank them all for their wisdom and generosity.

The descriptions below set out the several full cycles I endured over thirty years. This list encapsulates the stages of abuse *as I encountered them*—physically, mentally, and emotionally.

- *Love-bombing* is the abuser's way of reeling you in. His behavior is impeccable: he is polite, thoughtful, and attentive. He lavishes you with gifts, restaurant meals, trips—even when he can't afford these treats. He compliments you frequently and convinces you of his undying love and admiration. You may think this is too good to be true, and that's because it is. Keep in mind, though, that he's got you in his sights because he's figured out that you are vulnerable to his charms.
- *Devaluing* is what awaits you after you've fallen for his love-bombing hook, line, and sinker. Once you've been caught by this wonderful guy, he segues into contempt, unreasonableness, and often inexplicable ugliness. Inter alia, we're talking about forgetting to do stuff; refusing to cooperate with agreed upon arrangements; weighing in on matters that are none of

---

[7] Websites for the four professionals named above: www.doctor-ramani.com; www.unhookedmedia.com/todd-grande; www.commonego.com; and www.stephanielynlifecoaching.com.

his business; making not-very-funny jokes at your expense; issuing absurd demands; leveling major criticism or chucking stunning insults at you; denigrating your friends and family members; lying; calling you a liar; denying that he said or did something; denying that you said or did something; instigating huge arguments over minor matters; flustering you with a barrage of questions he gives you no opportunity to answer; screaming, swearing, and exploding without warning; conducting tirades that can last hours; preventing you from leaving a room; threatening to divorce you; threatening you physically; and then possibly slapping, pushing, kicking, or punching you or even pulling you down by your hair.

- *Discarding* is exactly what it sounds like: he is getting rid of you. It's the phase you should welcome because it's your chance to extricate yourself. However, during the previous phase, you've had your confidence severely dented and are in a constant state of confusion. You honestly think that what you have with him is love. You don't want the relationship to end, and oftentimes, he doesn't want it to end either. Because of his pathology, your abuser may want to have his cake and eat it too. Moreover, he is probably enjoying the chaos and upset he is causing. If you've been through a few cycles of abuse, you may no longer have the perspective to view the discarding as an opportunity to escape or have the constitution to do so. You might not know that you've been discarded, either because he's moved on without informing you or had an affair, which he may conceal or enjoy revealing to you after the fact. Even if he doesn't intend to actually leave you, his flirtations, dalliances, and affairs all count as discarding.
- *Hoovering* takes place when he's decided that discarding you was a bad idea. (He will also hoover when he recognizes the need to make amends for extreme devaluing that could drive you away.) He vacuums you up because he desperately needs you. He hasn't had an epiphany about your wonderful qualities or

learned the meaning of true love. No, he depends on your narcissistic supply—that is, the support you provide for his self-esteem and everyday functioning. And if you grow the cojones to discard him, he'll hoover you back up because he has the additional need to be the dumper rather than the dumpee. Just you wait.

You can depend on this cycle. It is "eternal," as Dr. Ramani explains. In my own experience, this was certainly true, but the stages of the cycle were never clearly delineated or uniform in style or length. No doubt, cycles of abuse reflect variations in individual natures and circumstances. Nevertheless, as a paradigm for understanding abuse, you should find the four-stage model invaluable. I wonder how different my life could have been if I'd known about the cycle of abuse earlier in my relationship, particularly during the twenty months it took the first full cycle to complete. At that juncture, I was hooked but not fully ground down. I was still capable of making decisions and might have acted in my own interest if I'd recognized Tom's abuse for what it was.

But as time went on and the next cycle began, I doubt I could have trusted my gut sufficiently to take terminal action even if I'd been educated about abuse. Abuse is mind-bending, confidence-depleting, and life-draining. You literally lose your *self*.

While I became keenly attuned to likely deteriorations in Tom's mood and adept at choosing my safest defense postures, I lost the capacity of an otherwise intelligent adult to see just how destructive and irredeemable the relationship dynamic was. I was hurt and perplexed by the ongoing and unexpected cruelty, desiring only to make things right. Because I considered myself the primary cause of Tom's irritation, anger, or loss of control, I was usually unable or unwilling to see his devaluing behavior as maltreatment.

After Tom's physical assaults—the only ones that truly counted as far as he was concerned—he would come up with grandiose hoover maneuvers that included earnest promises to change, maudlin protestations of love, and some of his tried-and-true love-bombing tricks. This chicanery duped me when Tom intended it to and then contributed to the confusion that accumulated over decades.

As mentioned, Tom broke up with me suddenly and without warning. Because we were working hard at our respective jobs and not living together, there was little interaction between us. I therefore had no inkling I was about to be discarded. In the absence of devaluing on Tom's part, I agonized over what could have happened and pined for him—but not for long. A month after the breakup, he returned in full force. I later learned that the reason for my discarding had been Tom's interest in a lovely new continental coworker, an attraction that was unrequited. With the French Filly out of contention, Tom was all in again, and I took him back with open arms. The cycle resumed.

As our relationship progressed, the abuse cycled in continuous loops, but the stages shortened, lengthened, morphed, and bled into each other as Tom became more emboldened, sophisticated—and unstable. For the remainder of our thirty-year relationship, the centrifuge of cruelty spun on, with Tom's principal goals being to assert dominance and keep me constantly off-balance. The result was constant mayhem in our relationship, which gave Tom a feeling of measurable progress akin to decreasing his handicap in golf.

Except for the episode I describe above, Tom's imminent discarding was directly preceded by masterful devaluing. In this stage, Tom had no interest in me except to shower me in stunning and unnecessary put-downs. (Unfortunately, he never embraced the silent treatment, which would've been merciful.) In retrospect, I know that discarding was *always* triggered by the appearance of another woman. The French Filly was only the first in a long line of distractions.

HARBINGER OF DISCARDING: TOM'S WANDERING EYE

I was usually unaware of the existence of the other woman at the time she was the focus of Tom's attention, although he occasionally pursued her right in front of me. This brazen behavior wasn't to taunt me; it was because he saw something he wanted more and felt entitled to it. It was as simple as that. The most flagrant example of Tom going after what he wanted happened when we were engaged.

I'd invited a former colleague, Alison, to take a European holiday with a group of us. From the moment of Alison's arrival, Tom made no effort to hide his interest in her. He was embarrassingly solicitous and smiled at her the way he'd smiled at me at the beginning of our courtship. When Alison almost caused us to miss our plane because of her laid-back attitude to packing, Tom couldn't have been more understanding. As she plopped her suitcase down on the platform at a French railway station to have a smoke, he sat down beside her to soothe her frazzled nerves and then offered to carry her suitcase. All of this transpired as we were dashing to connect with another train.

During discussions, he agreed with Alison's every utterance. Coming from me, ignorant comments such as "We have too many Iranian Jews in California, and they should all be shipped back!" would have been met with unequivocal chastisement from Tom. Instead, when I took issue with Alison's bigotry, Tom delivered this public admonishment: "Nunzia, Alison may be right. You should listen to her. You might learn something." Dear Reader, are you getting the picture?

Although I was deeply hurt by Tom's undisguised worship of Alison, my fear and diminished headspace prevented me from taking action. After she returned to the US—which abruptly ended Tom's romantic conquest—I mustered the courage to tell him how anxious and uncomfortable his behavior made me feel. He wasn't remotely contrite; in fact, he savaged me at high volume for what seemed like hours. *The entire scenario was a figment of my imagination, and I needed to stop making things up and causing trouble.*

Moral of the story: I should've taken advantage of the break we had shortly after the currency exchange place assault because when we got back together, Tom became increasingly adept at messing with my head—not only through his wandering eye, but also through many other cruelties and humiliations. He did what he wanted, reveled in crushing me, and prevailed in all situations.

Furthermore, Tom had to control the narrative as well as the situation. Therefore, he was often forced to abruptly and vehemently revise history. When he realized how poorly events reflected on him or that the truth put him at a disadvantage, he decided that none of this had ever happened, as he'd done with the Alison flirtation. As we leave this educational digression about the cycle of abuse and return to *Vignettes of Violence*, I can assure you that Tom's categorical denial of the shocking behavior I'm about to describe never moved me. I recall the disgrace in living color, as though it took place yesterday.

GET ME MY BOARDING PASS! I NEED MY FUCKING BOARDING PASS NOW!

Fast-forward to our first year of marriage. On the second leg of a trip to South America, we were at the airport, about to fly from Lima to Machu Picchu. When we made our way to the front of the line, the dour, unhelpful lady behind the desk informed me that the flight was leaving early. *Well, that's a first.* I speak Spanish, so I hadn't misunderstood. However, being a flexible person who didn't mind the vagaries and adventure of international travel, I figured (to myself, of course), *Well, if the flight is leaving early, we'll miss the plane, as will everybody behind us. No worries. We'll get to our destination at some point.*

I relayed the schedule change to Tom, who immediately erupted. I told him to keep it down. For valid historical reasons, Latin Americans aren't well disposed to *Yanquis*.

I stood silently at the counter for three minutes and asked again when the flight was leaving. Señora Sourpuss wouldn't look up from her computer. The steam was starting to come out of Tom's ears. "Ask her when we're leaving. Ask her why it's leaving early. Fucking hell! Ask her if we will get on this flight." His badgering became louder and more insistent. Because Tom didn't give a shit about cultural sensitivities, I couldn't get him to pipe down.

I used the politest Spanish to inquire yet again about the status of the flight. Señora Sourpuss still didn't respond. Nothing. Zilch. Nada. It must be acknowledged that, in any culture, this brand of customer service is out of order.

At this juncture, Tom had had enough. In great British tradition, he started off with a posh and indignant "You listen here!" and then banged his passport on the counter several times. His face was beet red, his shoulders were lifting and shaking, his lips were pursing and quivering, and he screamed louder than I'd ever heard anyone scream in a public place. "Get me my boarding pass. I need my fucking boarding pass now!" Tom's enunciation was impeccable, and the entire concourse stopped to enjoy the show.

Magically, the supervisor emerged from behind a one-way mirror to inform us in perfect American English that we wouldn't be flying on her airline because my husband had threatened her staff. Great! International travel had just become an even greater adventure! *OK, I need to find our baggage because we're now taking a twenty-four-hour bus ride to Machu Picchu.*

By virtue of being Tom's wife, I too was persona non grata. Consequently, none of the airline employees would tell me how to retrieve our luggage. I worked my way along the counter, my despair and panic growing at each window. When I got to the fellow at the very last window, I was genuinely in tears, wailing that my husband had been ill for several days. (This was almost true. He'd had two days of Montezuma's revenge thanks to the crab soufflé he'd eaten earlier in the trip despite my knowledgeable warning that this was a bad menu choice in the interior.) My damsel-in-distress act worked, and the fellow disappeared into the back office for a few minutes. He came out with the supervisor, who said to me, "OK, you can stay on this flight, but your husband will have to apologize to my employee."

It was both cringeworthy and extremely gratifying to watch

Tom grovel to Señora Sourpuss. We received our boarding passes and dashed to the gate, where we then waited an hour and a half. When we finally boarded in ignominy, the plane sat on the tarmac for a further forty-five minutes. All told, we departed two and a half hours behind schedule. *Whatever.*

Tom, in the bazillion times he recounted this story—until he stopped, denying it ever happened—used the sullenness, arrogance, and incompetence of the airline staff to justify his position that certain cultures, especially Hispanic ones, weren't ready for democracy but rather, needed strongmen to shepherd them into the future. Once they reached a later stage of development, perhaps they could be trusted to govern themselves. Tom, as both an Englishman and graduate in politics and economics from a second-rate university, felt particularly qualified to make such judgments.

I'M COMING HOME TO DEAL WITH YOU, BITCH

A couple decades later, when the kids were teenagers and away at boarding school and college, Tom—seemingly out of the blue on an otherwise unremarkable morning—became absolutely enraged during a phone call with me. We weren't arguing, and as far as my seismograph could detect, there were no tremors in the vicinity. Tom was in a good mood, which meant I could drop my guard a little and mention something that concerned me. I took the chance. Abruptly, Tom's demeanor changed and he erupted.

I registered the magnitude of the anger and outrage emanating from the receiver and had good reason to fear imminent physical violence when Tom announced he was coming home to deal with me. I didn't call the police because doing so would have likely resulted in severe consequences for Tom and, therefore, me and the kids—avoidance of severe consequences being one of my misguided priorities. Besides, the police were unlikely to show up preemptively to deal with an assailant who hadn't arrived, especially in our tony neighborhood.

The genesis of this major incident? I had the temerity to ask where Tom had found the specialist movers coming to crate our artwork in advance of our move to a bigger, better, absurdly opulent apartment. As sensitive as I was to Tom's seismic activity, I hadn't anticipated this response. But really, I should have: any question along these lines would have been perceived as a challenge to Tom's authority and superior wisdom. When the eruption occurred, I instantly went into appeasement mode. However, I should have also known that anything further from me would not only have been futile but would have also increased the flow of molten lava that couldn't be outrun.

Indeed, over the years, Tom's abuse had proliferated, escalated, matured, expanded, solidified, and covered the entire landscape. Dear Reader, if you'll allow me a bit more hyperbole and clumsy extended metaphor, the image I conjure up, especially for the final decade of our marriage, is of a massive, dark, impenetrable dome closing in on me as well as the kids. Tom frequently fortified this dome of personal totalitarianism with flows of magma from his constantly boiling, roiling insides that would harden into yet another layer of igneous rock.

Tom had become inordinately pleased with himself and didn't experience a scintilla of self-doubt on any matter, including the relentless instigating of his troublemaker wife. He needed no input, including questions, from a pea-brained cunt like me. After all, he'd done extremely well in his corporate career and then achieved undreamed of financial success and acclaim when he started his own business with a former colleague. Big Swinging Dicks, both of them:[8] unrivaled, untouchable, unimpeachable, entitled, extravagant, insufferable, arrogant, above-the-law.

Having left the house only an hour before with a smile on his face and a spring in his step, Tom, my very own Big Swinging Dick,

---

[8] The term *Big Swinging Dick*, from *Liar's Poker*, Michael Lewis's 1989 exposé of Wall Street excesses, refers to financial executives who generate enormous profits. This moniker, which appears to have fallen out of fashion, was generally received as a compliment but was not always given that way.

was irate that I had the audacity to ask a question about a decision he'd made and that I wasn't retracting it or apologizing—both of which, of course, I was scrambling to do. He wasn't buying it, and I needed to be punished for my insubordination. He was leaving work and coming home to put his bitch of a wife in her place. As I said, I knew he meant it. With our housekeeper on vacation, I had no recourse or protection.

I made the snap decision to call Annabel, Tom's business partner's wife, making this only the second time I'd revealed to anyone outside Tom's family the abuse I was subjected to. I grabbed my cell phone, ran into my daughter's room, locked the door, and dialed. I figured Annabel could at least be a phone witness to whatever happened and hoped she'd immediately call her husband, Piers, who'd be able to persuade Tom to stand down. Needless to say, Annabel had no idea what I was on about as I sobbed down the line.

Immediately upon hanging up from our ill-fated phone call, Tom must have grabbed his car keys and gone down to the parking bay to get into his newly acquired toy, the fastest production sports car available. He must have then encountered no traffic as he sped to our home. (More on his driving in Chapter 9.) He was home within ten minutes and soon located me in the locked bedroom. He demanded I open the fucking door. He screamed. He swore. He threatened. He banged the door with his fists. He kicked it repeatedly with his shoe. All this over a question I'd asked about a specialty moving company.

When Annabel heard Tom in this uncontrollable rage, she understood why I'd called and she, too, began to cry. As Tom's fury escalated, I thought he'd succeed in banging the door in. With the cell phone wedged between my chin and shoulder, I managed to shove heavy furniture up against the door just in case he did. After fifteen minutes of this violence, Tom gave up and returned to the office. Not a moment too soon because Annabel had heard enough and was about to put me on hold to call Piers and the police.

The police were never notified about this incident. I suspect that Piers had a brief word with Tom to advise him to dial it down. (No doubt Piers was chiefly concerned about the reputational risk Tom's behavior posed for the business.) Neither Piers nor Annabel ever broached the topic of this horrifying incident with me, almost certainly because they didn't want to wade into the middle and possibly because they didn't want to cause me further distress. Whatever the reason, I'd have taken comfort from knowing people cared enough to ask how they might help.

For my part, I was so traumatized by this most recent episode in Tom's triumphant season of devaluing—extreme, constant, protracted—that I packed my bags and checked into a hotel as I pondered what to do next. This was the first time in fifteen years that I'd had the gumption to exit Tom's dome. Unfortunately, it wasn't the last time I would allow myself to be lured back by his manipulation and empty promises to change.

CHAPTER 2

THE OFFICE

I'M NOT INTERESTED IN OFFICE POLITICS

When Tom started his career, he was able to keep his temper under control in the office. He was incredibly grateful for the investment banking job I'd procured for him through my alumni and professional connections—a last-minute reprieve from the poorly paid government agency job he'd accepted in the north of England. His London colleagues were jovial, and this was a heady time to be working in finance. Tom felt he was finally on the trajectory someone of his talent and intelligence deserved. He hadn't yet developed the sense of superiority and entitlement that would become his undoing, but he was already an operator determined to get what he wanted through any means.

I can now acknowledge that Tom, for all his proclaimed morality, honesty, and dislike of office politics, was a skilled, dogged political animal from the get-go. It was right in front of me, and I didn't see it. Within a year of starting his first job, through some cunning upward management, he arranged for his boss to be transferred to a less important location but with the same job title as a sop. The endgame: to get his boss's job.

Tom succeeded and, with incredible aplomb, got other future colleagues shuffled, fired, or demoted, or merely tarnished their reputations, whatever was required to fulfill his objectives. Some of Tom's victims were bitter. Some are still unaware of Tom's instrumental role in their demise. I'm ashamed to say that, as a devoted wife, I eagerly and unquestioningly lapped up Tom's accounts of the incompetent and malicious bastards he had to work with. Some of them were nasty pieces of work, for sure. Others seemed like perfectly decent and diligent fellows who just happened to get in Tom's way.

In our first overseas posting, which came only three years after Tom started his career, he landed a very high position, with the salary and outrageous benefits of such an exalted role, including club memberships and an enormous, beautiful apartment in the best neighborhood.

When we got settled in, I suggested we invite couples we'd met at business dinners, which was our only avenue to meeting people at first. Tom's answer was always a resounding and hostile *no*: "I'm not a whore like my other colleagues, and I won't invite people I don't like [salesmen and clients] into my home." It was the same attitude when I suggested inviting his colleagues. He didn't like them and didn't want to spend any more time with them than was necessary. On top of his refusal to cooperate, Tom was duty-bound to savage me for the mere mention of a social gathering. I have no specific insights as to why Tom behaved this way; however, I now know that people with BPD are characterized by sudden unreasonable behavior, including making unfavorable snap judgments of others and demanding that their partners share their views.

I should have been more concerned by Tom's hostility and antisocial attitude, but I was merely frustrated because he hadn't been that way in London. And why had we packed our wedding china, a full set of handblown crystal chosen by Tom himself, and his family's silver if we didn't intend on using it? We didn't even have to worry about preparing the food; we had a full-time housekeeper who was a fantastic cook.

I went ahead and organized some small soirees with acquaintances Tom hadn't blacklisted outright. Lo and behold, and without forewarning, he dropped his antisocial attitude—quickly reversing judgments and refusing all discussions of U-turns is another BPD trait—and took the initiative to invite business contacts, colleagues, and all their wives to dinner. It was now Tom's idea to socialize, you see. Within a year, we were ensconced in the expat whirl and hosting dinners at an alarming rate.

During this posting, which lasted almost six years, Tom had little time or respect for me. In fact, this was a period of frequent verbal and physical abuse and almost nightly mini-explosions from Tom. Interestingly, though, he openly admired me for my ability to make friends with all and sundry. He named me "the Connector" and meant it as a genuine compliment. In social situations, he imitated my behavior and speech. I occasionally overheard him parroting my exact words, with the same tone and cadence.

Of course, I never dared comment on my observations because I didn't want to ruin a good thing or cause trouble. In fact, I viewed this development in a positive light and perceived it as an authentic desire to change. I believed Tom finally recognized that he was hurting himself with his snobbery and ever-present hostility. While Tom did learn some lessons about dealing with others in social and professional situations, I now know that another feature of BPD sufferers is the tendency to mimic others to fill in their own unstable, empty identities.

It's unspeakably sad that Tom was so uncomfortable in his own skin that he needed to be taught how to relate. It's even sadder that he hasn't reaped the benefits of a winning personality and genuine interest in others. Indeed, true connection appears to have mainly eluded Tom. Of course, Tom has mates, folks he considers friends. For Tom's sake, I hope they appreciate him for his brilliance and generosity and reciprocate whatever affection he feels for them.

ARREST FOR ASSAULT

In the office environment, Tom had always been appreciated, by his underlings at least, for his congeniality and fabulous generosity. However, in the incandescent heat of his own successful enterprise, he became known for his unstable temper, which he'd generally done a good job of concealing throughout his two decades of corporate roles.[9] Thanks to Tom's indiscriminate and unpredictable eruptions, everyone, including the rank and file, was becoming wary of him.

Tom often had run-ins with his business partner, Piers, in front of the entire office, some of them so bad that all eyes were glued to their screens and no one budged from their desk until the ruckus was over. One of the performances was so extreme that Piers took Tom aside to tell him there'd be ramifications if he ever lost control like that again. Tom was suitably chastened and perhaps even felt a modicum of shame for upsetting and embarrassing everyone who had to witness his meltdown.

However, Tom was already on a dangerous path, one that some people familiar with him have called a "death wish," brought about by a midlife crisis and ever-growing feelings of entitlement superimposed on his cluster B personality. Massive porn consumption, wide-ranging and frequent sexual activity, alcohol (probably enhanced by party drugs), and the dubious company he kept were causes as well as symptoms of his mangled psyche, with everything feeding into the loop of craziness and violence.

One evening in the late spring, Tom went out to dinner with an old industry mate. The talk turned to politics, and I think it's safe to say that both fellows were well oiled at this point. Like most

---

[9] The one exception was Tom's appalling behavior in a corporate job he deemed merely a "parking place." He was wholly uncooperative with colleagues and downright disrespectful toward management, accusing two of his bosses of being criminals. He jumped just as he was about to be pushed. Too bad. It was an open secret that the firm was about to be acquired. If Tom had stayed another month, the European colossus that bought it would have handed him a year's bonus to stay or a hefty payment to leave. This is just one example of Tom's instability causing him to cut off his nose to spite his face. I was obviously expected to fully support Tom's decision.

of us, Tom's emotions were heightened by too much alcohol, but because of his instability, the effect of several bottles of vino capped off by some single malt was even more pronounced.

The match in the powder keg was Tom's firm conviction that the US and Britain had been completely justified in prosecuting the second Gulf War. Saddam Hussein *had to go*, despite conclusive evidence that Saddam didn't have Weapons of Mass Destruction. Tom was never one to let facts get in the way of his stance.

His mate, also very successful and at least as well educated, had the nerve to disagree with Tom, who, even when sober, felt unassailable on the subject of global affairs thanks to his aforementioned degree in politics and economics. Apparently, there was an unpleasant set-to in the restaurant.

In an outraged state, Tom parted from his mate and went back to the office to check the markets, pick up his briefcase, and turn off the lights, whereupon he headed down to street level to hail a taxi in front of his building. One of the building's female night janitors blithely wandered in front of Tom and grabbed the first taxi that passed by. Goodness knows who the oblivious party was. Tom, though, was sure it wasn't him. Apoplectic with rage, he lunged directly in front the woman to physically prevent her from opening the door to the taxi. As Tom proceeded to berate this "inconsiderate peasant" at high volume, the taxi driver made the rational decision to keep going. While Tom would have used his arms to block the woman's movement, I don't believe he struck her.

Nevertheless, this was a horrifying act of violence. Having been on the receiving end of Tom's meltdowns on hundreds of occasions, I can well imagine how scared and angry this woman felt with Tom flailing his arms and brandishing his briefcase directly in front of her and shrieking literally in her face. She immediately called the police, and Tom had the presence of mind to stay. As a major tenant of the building, he was eminently traceable.

The police arrived and arrested Tom for assault.

At 1:30 a.m., I received the call to come bail him out. I got to the police station with the bail money as soon as I could, but Tom had to stay a bit longer to be processed. I went home and managed to get back to sleep only with the help of a tranquilizer.

When I woke up the next day to the reality of the night before, I was traumatized. I worried about a conviction. I worried that even without a conviction, press coverage would mean the end of Tom's career. I worried about what would happen to my family and, in particular, my children. In hindsight, I can see I was worried about all the wrong things, the misguided priorities I wrote of earlier. It may not have worked, but I should have attempted to use this incident to force Tom to face his problems and get some help.

Along with Tom, I'd lost the plot. Where was my good judgment? My own moral bearings? I was unwilling to wrap my head around the full extent of Tom's problem, and the previous two decades had made me feel utterly powerless in effecting any sort of change in him.

In a nutshell, I was scared of confronting Tom, and I was scared of confronting my fear. I knew from past experience that pushing him too far or making him feel bad about anything would only lead to incensed justification from him, more punishment for me, and absolutely no constructive outcome for our marriage. Tom was a law unto himself.

After I fled with the three kids when they were very young, Tom promised to get psychiatric help if I returned. I returned, and we reconciled. Tom never got around to making any appointments and quickly reverted to type. Indeed, he later taunted me with the insincerity of his erstwhile promise: *psychiatry was bullshit and he'd never intended to do as he promised.* There was nothing I could do to counter his unabashed hypocrisy and deceit.

It is now glaringly obvious to me that Tom's guiding principle in the realm of human interaction was what Patricia Evans, in her book *The Verbally Abusive Relationship*, terms "power over," an unbridled and unshakable sense of dominion over others.[10] During my marriage, I was well and truly stuck in Tom's reality.

Consequently, I followed the path of least resistance, harboring the private but delusional hope that this assault arrest would go away and that, off his own bat, Tom would do some much-needed self-examination and get into therapy.

First things first, though. Tom had to deal with this serious legal problem. He immediately engaged our town's most skilled criminal lawyer, known for being able to finesse both police and prosecutor. Unfortunately, the prosecutor wasn't up for any finessing this time around. Tom's lawyer made a settlement offer to the victim, but the prosecutor was so angry about Tom's entitled behavior that he refused to present the offer to the victim.

We had to prepare for trial. I had the ignominious task of going to my pastor to ask for a character reference for Tom, which he very kindly gave. Tom wasn't involved enough at church to ask for this himself. I was also ordered by Tom to rack my brain to come up with all the charitable endeavors he'd been involved in. Let's just say it was an embellished litany because Tom had done very little "giving back."

It was a terrible summer and fall. The waiting and worry made me physically ill. I prayed constantly, which was the source of some comfort. But I had no one to talk to, and, quite frankly, I was too mortified to divulge this shameful incident to anyone. Of course, we kept this news from the kids as well. Tom was contrite and somewhat nicer to me, but the two of us were assiduously avoiding the subject. There was no discussion of the professional ramifications of conviction or the effect on our family of losing our livelihood or the lasting damage to our children of having a father with a criminal record—and possibly in prison. No discussion of

---

10   Evans distinguishes between the totalitarian spirit of "power over" and the "mutuality and co-creation" of "personal power," whereby loving, nurturing people do not feel the need to exert control over others. Patricia Evans, *The Verbally Abusive Relationship* (Adams Media, 2010).

the screaming necessity of dealing with the deep-seated causes of such god-awful behavior. No discussion of the likelihood that such a loss of control could happen again, resulting in serious harm to another person.

I don't know how Tom functioned. He appeared unconcerned, perhaps because he had faith that his expensive lawyer would finagle a solution. I know that I pushed myself through each day, grateful that the kids were away at school for most of the ordeal. Together, we succeeded in pretending the whole thing away until it was time for the hearing.

When the day came, I was instructed how to dress and conduct myself. I'd written a note in the victim's language, telling her how sorry I was about my husband's actions. I added that he was a good family man and that I hoped for her generosity and forgiveness. I had this note at the ready along with a large bouquet of flowers. As for Tom, he had a wad of cash in his suit pocket—just in case.

Right before the scheduled hearing, Tom's lawyer ran from the court to where we were waiting outside. The victim had accepted a financial settlement to withdraw her charges! Let's just say this poor, unsophisticated woman was robbed. She had no idea that she could have demanded fifty times the amount and Tom would have paid. He'd already made the calculation for this horse trade.

Needless to say, this near hit didn't change Tom's behavior. While he'd been more tractable during the months of waiting, he became nasty, unpleasant, unpredictable Tom again upon the settlement. He quickly dismissed this serious incident from his mind. If he ever thinks about it at all, I'm sure he still considers the female janitor at fault for his meltdown—because he was waiting for the taxi first, and there is absolutely no way he is mistaken about this. How dare anybody not show him the deference due him? Tom was, and is, a Big Swinging Dick who just has a little anger management problem. He has no idea that Anger is, in fact, a huge and ever-present entity in his life, one he welcomes, enjoys, and cultivates.

YOU FUCKWIT

Of course I knew about Tom's arrest and meltdowns with Piers in front of everyone at the office. It was only in the final year of our marriage that I learned that others working in his business, namely *women*, were now enduring his escalating abuse. Tom boasted to me that he'd sharply and publicly rebuked his diligent, long-serving office manager for not completing a particular task to his exacting standards. He informed one secretary, in no uncertain terms, that she needed to start dressing properly. Tom gleefully reported, "She didn't like it very much!" He really let her have it, no doubt leaving her humiliated and angry.

Early one evening during a boarding school break, our daughter and nephew, who'd been studying together at Tom's office for their big exams, came home for a workout before supper. My daughter was clearly down, and she burst into tears when I asked her what was wrong. She explained that while she and her cousin were studying in the boardroom, Tom had berated Renata, a female trader, for buying the wrong quantity of a futures contract. Tom's constructive solution to Renata's error was to scream at her for twenty minutes in front of the whole office, repeatedly calling her a "fuckwit." Renata, though tough as old boots, fled the office in tears. The kids could hear all the action, even with the boardroom doors closed, and our daughter was understandably ashamed. Of course, Tom didn't mention a thing when he got home that evening. For him, it had probably been a typical day at the office.

When I ran into Renata after my split from Tom, I told her how embarrassed I'd been to learn about this incident. I hadn't known how to deal with it, so had done nothing. Renata said she didn't know what I was talking about. I reacted with disbelief that she'd forgotten such an incident. She replied that she hadn't forgotten. She just didn't know *which* incident I was referring to because Tom lambasting her in front of the entire office had become a frequent occurrence. She'd fled the office in tears more than once.

She reassured me that I didn't need to be sorry. In fact, she told me the staff had speculated, *If Tom is behaving this way at the office, how must he behave toward Nunzia in private?*

Yes, I'd done an excellent job of hiding my plight from the outside world for the entirety of our relationship. It was only when Tom began to unravel conspicuously at the office that it occurred to his colleagues that I—strong, smart, confident Nunzia—might be suffering at home.

Long story short, the burden of Tom's hatred of me and the double life he led (which you will read about in my final chapters) exploded his business as well as his home life, ruptures that surprised even his closest colleagues.

CHAPTER 3

MISTREATMENT OF OUR CHILDREN

MR. ENTERTAINMENT

Tom was a loving and devoted father to our children, Dominic, Louisa, and Jamie. He read to them, took them on fabulous excursions, and bought them anything they asked for. I was at the coalface, dealing with the gamut of practical problems: making sure the homework got done, orchestrating activities and tutors, getting the boys to ice hockey at 5:15 a.m. so I could lace up skates to their exacting standards, assisting with the completion of school projects that were due without fail on Monday morning, dealing with housemasters when discipline problems cropped up, and hopping on planes to handle more serious issues.

I was the enforcer and factotum, while Tom was Mr. Entertainment. On the face of it, our household arrangements were no different from those in many families operating according to traditional gender roles. Unfortunately, our family dynamic had another constant: the ever-present disrespect and abuse of the mother by the father, from the time each child was born, and sometimes even before.

Simply put, abuse of the mother amounts to abuse of the children. Children witnessing abuse experience deep anxiety. They speculate on the causes and sometimes blame themselves. They worry about what could happen next. Depending on the frequency and severity of abuse, children can develop physical illnesses, learning disabilities, low self-esteem, and PTSD. Many children living in the midst of spousal abuse encounter severe challenges with social interaction and often respond aggressively to episodes they perceive as threatening. Some children receive the message that the victimized parent deserves what she gets and join in the cruelty. For a comprehensive look at the effects of spousal abuse on children, I refer you to Alison Cunningham and Linda Baker's 2007 report for Canada's Centre for Children and Families in the Justice System, *Little Eyes, Little Ears: How Violence Against a Mother Shapes Children as They Grow*.[11]

You may wonder, therefore, why I didn't stand up to Tom to protect my children from this indirect but pernicious form of abuse. Why didn't I just up and leave with the children? As mentioned, I did manage once, early on, to flee the house undetected with all three kids, after a spectacular loss of control by Tom when he punished me for the cumulative sins of his underlings, colleagues, and bosses. I was in a foreign country with no resources of my own, and Tom was able to entice me back with the promise that he'd never lose his shit like that again and that he'd attend therapy with one of the many English-speaking psychiatrists available in our locale. However, with each year, Tom became more brazen and menacing, and I became more afraid. If I left him, he'd divorce me, sue for full custody of the kids, win, and leave me in penury.

---

[11] Alison Cunningham and Linda Baker, *Little Eyes, Little Ears: How Violence Against a Mother Shapes Children as They Grow* (Centre for Children and Families in the Justice System, 2007), www.canada.ca/en/public-health/services/health-promotion/stop-family-violence/prevention-resource-centre/women/little-eyes-little-ears-violence-against-a-mother-shapes-children-they-grow.html.

I'm sure of this because he told me so. After yet another unnecessary and extremely unpleasant argument, this time in our second posting, Tom literally shoved me out of the apartment as Louisa watched, shaking and bewildered. He told me not to show my face again and informed me that I'd soon be hearing from the nastiest divorce lawyer in town. He'd get the kids and I'd get nothing. With that horrifying threat (but no handbag or coat), I made my way to a friend's place, where Tom finally located me after two days and convinced me to come back yet again.

This demonstration of my ongoing spinelessness dovetails neatly into my misguided reasons for not going through with divorce despite meeting with three divorce lawyers over the years. First, I objected to divorce as a product of sin. Second, I considered divorce a shameful personal failure as both wife and mother, a selfish route a woman of my upbringing couldn't countenance. Third, and probably most important, I worried about the lifelong ramifications of divorce for Dominic, Louisa, and Jamie, even if I did win custody.

I needed to persist with Tom, and almost to the bitter end I suffered from the delusion that, any day now, gentle words and logic would convince him to gain sovereignty over himself. Yes, Tom could become a constant and loving husband and father! Other women who've been in the same situation will understand that my overweening instinct was to preserve the family in the hope that Tom would soon have an epiphany, allowing family life to morph into an episode of *The Waltons*. As I said earlier, I'll carry my guilt to the grave.

A BAD START IN LIFE

When Dominic was two, we decided we wanted another child. To this end, we took a romantic weekend at a divine resort a short plane ride away from our posting. Despite Tom's constant impatience, the low-grade fever I was accustomed to dealing with daily, it was a lovely weekend. On Sunday, we had a return flight at 2:30 p.m. When Tom told me he'd booked the very expensive hotel car for noon, I suggested we take the airport shuttle instead. It was leaving only fifteen minutes earlier and cost a fraction of the fancy hotel car. I didn't insist. I merely made a suggestion, as a peer or colleague might. Tom instantly went berserk: "I work hard and deserve to relax, and I'll book a car if I like." He lunged toward me so wild with fury that he was spitting on me as he screamed.

As I cowered on the far corner of the bed, I asked him to please stop screaming and spitting. *Bam!* He landed a punch in my left eye. It had turned green by the time we left for the airport (in the hotel car, of course), and by the time we got home, it was black. Yet again, I had to stay indoors for more than a week so no one would see me. I'm sure that Louisa was conceived that weekend away because I didn't want Tom to come near me for the next several weeks—not that he tried.

I started to feel unwell, and, lo and behold, I had a bun in the oven. Just after my pregnancy was confirmed, Monica, a dear friend who'd recently divorced, arrived for a long visit. Monica and Tom began experiencing friction a few weeks into her stay. On one occasion, it became a three-way argument as I tried to calm things down between them. Although it wasn't Tom's intention to knock me down, he pushed me, and I fell. As I lay on the floor, I kept my eyes closed and my arms clasped around my head. I remember thinking, *I'm not getting up because I want him to stop yelling.* He didn't stop. After savaging Monica some more, he barked at me, "Get the fuck up. There's nothing wrong with you." Then he gave me a sharp kick in the rear end. At least he didn't kick me in the stomach.

I'll always wonder if Louisa's extreme anxiety and delayed speech had anything to do with the ongoing abuse I received from the moment of her conception. Fortunately, she has successfully conquered her communication problems; however, she continues to suffer from bouts of anxiety. And, from my perspective, her relationship choices strongly suggest an overwhelming need for quiet and stability rather than the fulfillment that comes from true love.

THE KID BLOODY WELL DESERVED IT!

Dominic was also a direct target of Tom's abuse, a revelation that will make you think even less of me for not leaving. One incident was so extreme that this sweet, forgiving boy will never be rid of the deep psychic wounds Tom inflicted. Hardly a day goes by that the memory doesn't plague me.

Some eight years after the black eye sustained on the weekend of Louisa's conception, we took a short family vacation in Provence. Upon our arrival at the tiny airport, ten-year-old Dominic took charge of one of the luggage trolleys. He was mucking around, not paying attention, and hit Tom in the back of the ankles with his cart. Tom immediately saw red. Who can blame him for getting angry? Being whacked by a luggage trolley is extremely painful, and Dominic needed to be severely reprimanded.

However, this isn't what happened. Tom went into furious mode. I recognized it immediately but was powerless to prevent what was about to go down. Tom's face became beet red and contorted in rage. His lips were pursed, sucked almost completely into his mouth. His shoulders began their customary lifting and falling and his whole body began to convulse, as it did whenever he became enraged. He then accelerated down the ramp toward the luggage carousel. At speed, Tom rammed his own trolley into Dominic's ankles.

The child cried out in agony and turned around to see what had just happened. Dominic saw that his own father, still wild with anger, had done this to him. The kid is tough, but he sobbed—not just because of the physical pain but also from the horror of realizing his own father had exacted revenge on him. The profound hurt and bewilderment on Dominic's face is seared onto my heart.

For once, I went into mama bear mode without trepidation,

but knew I had to wait until the kids were out of earshot. When we made it down the ramp, I told the kids to go to the carousel to look out for our luggage. I went behind a pillar and motioned Tom over. I informed him in a firm, even, businesslike tone that he'd never treat one of my children that way again, ever.

Was Tom chastened? Au contraire. The first words out of his mouth were, "Don't tell me what to do." This was followed by the claim that the kid bloody well deserved it. *Seriously? The kid deserved to be rammed in the back of the ankles by your trolley?* I told Tom I believed it was child abuse and absolutely the wrong message. It must never happen again. Full stop. Tom continued to argue the toss. No feeling of shame, no taking on board that he'd behaved vindictively and unconstructively. Just justification, justification, justification. I knew I was defeated. Tom was going to prevail in all things, and, more to the point, I had three kids in tow in a foreign country where I didn't speak the language. What further measures could I have taken?

If I'd committed such an act of violence, I'd have been bollocked then and there and for the rest of the holiday. Indeed, despite his poor memory, Tom would have retained this crime to rebuke me forever. As it was, the trolley incident emboldened Tom to be more dictatorial than usual during our week in Provence.

It wasn't the first time Dominic had suffered at Tom's hands. Several years earlier, Dominic had patches of skin removed from the top of his right hand because Tom was angry that we hadn't been out the door sooner. You see, it was a Sunday (see Chapter 4), and Tom had been taking it easy, lounging in bed, reading the *Financial Times*, being served toast and tea, when, all of a sudden, he thought to himself that we'd whiled away too much time at home. He decreed, "It's time to get out of the house."

I struggled to get ready with no help at all from Tom. Dominic and Louisa were good because they knew when Daddy meant business, but I still had to get myself and the baby's stuff ready. Tom grabbed the car keys and rushed out ahead of us. From the elevator lobby, he screamed for us and the neighbors to hear, "What the fuck is taking you so long?"

Not getting instantaneous compliance, Tom swore and stomped back to the apartment. He then pushed the front door open with tremendous force, even though he had just passed Dominic sitting in the doorway, attempting to get his shoes on. Dominic's hands were inconveniently in the way of Tom's shit fit, and the metal bottom of the door careened over Dominic's right hand. The poor kid tried to be brave, but it was painful and bloody. I wasn't given the chance to dress the wound before going out. I could only rinse it off and quickly wrap it in paper towels.

When we got back from our compulsory fun afternoon out, I gave the hand a good cleaning, put some disinfectant ointment and bandages on it, and kissed it better. But how could I kiss better the psychological wound of having your daddy, whom you love so much, thoughtlessly injure you because he had to get anger off his chest?

These two childhood incidents, along with verbal attacks you'll read about in Chapter 12, have made Dominic, now in his early thirties, determined to secure his father's love. Dominic was never going to be in the way again, literally or figuratively. To this day, he executes Tom's commands with alacrity and precision and appears to do whatever he can to stay in his father's good graces.

VENI, VIDI, VICI

Tom had always been imperious, but, as mentioned, his need to throw his weight around and lord it over others increased with age and success. One day, he was home early from work and unilaterally decided we needed to eat supper immediately. Jamie, our youngest, was at Latin tutoring in preparation for boarding school.

We asked Dominic to pop out with the driver to pick Jamie up. Upon arriving at the tutor's house, Dominic was unable to find his little brother, who should have been waiting outside, and called to tell me that. Tom became extremely cross and accused Dominic of being stupid and lazy. He ordered me to call Dominic back to tell him to fucking well find his brother and get home immediately. I conveyed a neutral version of the message. As we waited, Tom continued to fulminate about Dominic's fucking carelessness and what a moron he was.

I tentatively suggested that we didn't yet know what had happened, reminding Tom that Jamie was a bit absent-minded. He could well have gone back inside the tutor's house. I should have known no good would come out of me trying to defend one of the kids. Tom had already issued his verdict.

Tom turned on me with rage. "Don't you dare contradict me! When I say he's careless, he is."

Tom was about to embark on a roll. My attempts to mollify him were seen as further "contradiction." His tirade had to follow its natural course and burn out in its usual protracted way. Every time I offered conciliatory responses when Tom was in this mode, he'd do one or more of the following:

1. ignore what I said;
2. deflect with an unrelated insult;
3. call me a liar;
4. send rapid-fire questions in my direction, giving me no chance to respond;
5. demand to know why I was starting an argument;
6. descend into character assassination;
7. deny what he'd just said;
8. deny that I said what I'd said earlier;
9. scream more loudly;
10. threaten to divorce me and take the kids away;
11. threaten me physically; or
12. punch, slap, or manhandle me in some way.

For thirty years, I tried to figure out how I could deal with Tom differently. How I could form my sentences more simply, more logically, more articulately, and less vexingly so that he'd understand me better. How I could apologize and retract my words in ways that would satisfy him. How I could avoid making him angry in the first place. How I could be more pleasing as a wife. I put all the responsibility for solving an unsolvable problem on myself.

I read books on communication. I listened to podcasts on improving "disappointing" marriages. I implemented what Tom said he wanted. I snapped to when he issued an order. I prayed. Every once in a while, after a two-hour savaging, I'd scream, swear back, and stand up for myself. Otherwise, I limited my responses to the issue at hand. Not once did I make an ad hominem attack, insult his looks or intelligence, assassinate his character, call him a liar, deflect his remarks, gaslight him, or mess with his head in any way. My principled stance on fighting was all for naught, though. I needed a new approach.

A few months before the Latin lesson, a new approach had come in the form of guidance from Charlene, a Christian counselor recommended to us by the very discreet friend who took me in the first time I'd fled the house on my own. Charlene instructed me to refuse to discuss an issue until "both of us" had calmed down, but I was never given the choice by Tom, who needed to finish every argument and prevail. When that didn't work, Charlene advised me to walk away, but I was physically prevented from doing so by Tom. She admonished me to try harder at being a Christian wife. I should always be nicely put together when Tom got home. She needed me to be affectionate to Tom even after he'd savaged me. Nothing—not my spruced-up appearance, my self-abnegation, or my hugs and kisses—made a blind bit of difference to the frequency, duration, or degree of Tom's meltdowns. Convinced of her rightness and my bad attitude, Charlene then got me to read—and reread and do homework on—Gary Chapman's possibly well-intentioned but, in my view, dangerous and misogynistic self-help book for couples,

The 5 Love Languages, which the cunning Tom soon weaponized against me.[12] Nevertheless, I was so desperate that I slavishly persisted for almost two years with the entire litany of sexist and wrongheaded principles for Christian wives.

I'm fairly certain that Jesus condemns the subjugation and abuse of women by men. Indeed, it must be sinful in His eyes. Let me take this opportunity to caution all abused partners about faith-based counselors and resources pushing social or religious agendas that might not have your safety and happiness in mind.

The fact is, I lived with Tom's constant sharpness and impatience. On several occasions, including during counseling, Tom said without remorse that he wasn't really going to be able to change those aspects of himself. (In any case, I'd already normalized this daily assault on my psyche.) Furthermore, Tom was certain that I exaggerated his impatience and overstated his tendency to melt down. He therefore insisted that I accept the gamut of bad behaviors and instead focus on his good points! Tom believed his extreme generosity, which was what he determined I wanted and not what I myself wanted, trumped all his bad behavior. In calm moments, I tried to explain to him that I didn't want jewelry, watches, or fancy vacations. I'd much rather have a peaceful life in which the simplest daily transactions weren't fraught with danger. I told Tom the best gift he could give me was to choose to have a happy marriage and family life—not to see malice, thoughtlessness, or incompetence in my every action or utterance. He listened but didn't hear.

The accumulation of my failed efforts to change myself sufficiently and convince Tom that I wasn't trying to cause trouble appeared to only increase and harden his justified rage. As our marriage progressed (with the exceptions of his brief stint as a "Christian" husband and a couple times when he recognized he'd sent me to the brink), Tom became a conniving, dogged, malev-

---

12 Gary Chapman, *The 5 Love Languages: The Secret to Love That Lasts* (Northfield, 2015).

olent beast whose words and actions clearly communicated the subtext *Nunzia, no matter what you do, I will crush and vanquish you.*

I didn't understand until far too late that there was no way to avoid nastiness and trauma. There was nothing I could have said or done because Tom had already determined the outcome, thereby assuring himself of victory over me. Even when I did exactly as he demanded, he was fleet of foot in changing the goalposts to ensure that I'd fail. He'd always have something to be angry about. *That was his objective.*

For Tom, it wasn't about love. It was about defeating another person, someone he claimed to love. Tom's focus was on Tom. He considered himself a sensitive soul whose anger needed to be understood and tolerated because it was a reflection of his fear and fragility. In a rare moment of honesty about his emotional condition, Tom told me, "You need to understand, Nunzia. I have a lot of anger and am acting on it because I'm delicate. I'm badly hurt." Too bad for the rest of us. We clearly had no claim to fear, fragility, impatience, anger, or even justified irritation. And Tom certainly didn't care about the damage he caused when he hurt us. Indeed, while he could express his lifetime of hurt in any extreme way he wanted, our children and I had to swallow the hurt he inflicted on us because we couldn't risk the consequences of stoking his wrath.

Meanwhile, back at the Latin lesson, Jamie had gone back into the tutor's house to get something he'd forgotten. That's why he wasn't waiting outside when the driver arrived with Dominic to pick him up. The facts no longer mattered, though, because by the time the boys got back, Tom was in a complete state. As they walked through the door, I was literally backed into a corner trembling with fear while Tom bashed me verbally into complete submission.

Tom quickly turned his rage on the entire family, and within seconds, all of us were making a dash into the boys' room, with Tom in hot pursuit. Tom was able to barge through us to get into the room first. He knocked a bookshelf over and pushed one of the boys aside so that he could get a clear shot at me. All three kids were screaming and crying, and, as Tom slapped me, Dominic reached into the fray to give his father a shove.

Somehow, a shove from his son had a salutary effect on Tom, but of course, he had to have the last word to let us know we were in the wrong and he was boss. My abiding memory of this evening is Louisa wailing, "I never thought I'd see my father hit my mother." She knew about the screaming, yelling, ranting, and raving, and had seen Tom push me out the door, but she'd never seen him reach out to strike me in the face. It wouldn't be the last time, though.

CHAPTER 4

MANIC SUNDAY

NO TIP FOR POOR SERVICE

Sunday evening was our time for sitting with trays in front of the television. I did all the waiting, bussing, and popping up and down to get second helpings, drinks, and ketchup. Usually, I got effusive thanks for my service. One evening, however, I mistakenly removed the tray from Tom's lap because he'd positioned his cutlery to indicate he was finished. He wasn't, though, and the instant I took the tray he shrieked at me indignantly, "What the hell do you think you're doing?"

I was taken aback, not by my error in judgment but by Tom's shocking response. His nastiness was especially surprising given his insistence on good table manners. He could have said, "Oh, sorry, Darling, I'm not finished quite yet." When I apologized and explained I'd misunderstood, he wasn't placated. He berated me in front of the kids for the duration of the movie they were watching. I didn't muster the courage to retort, "I'm waiting on you hand and foot. That's what the hell I'm doing."

Yes, Sunday evenings had something special about them, a magical quality I never quite pinned down. Whether Tom was sitting in the lap of luxury at home being waited on by a devoted wife or enjoying the fabulous facilities of the various clubs we belonged to, Sunday evening frequently presented the occasion for him to completely lose it. Maybe it was the prospect of the week ahead, the need to visit on me the anticipated sins of his colleagues. All I know is that over three decades, many a Sunday evening ended in an eruption over seemingly nothing at all.

FACING THE MUSIC—JUST NOT WHEN I EXPECTED TO

One early Sunday evening when the kids were small, we were heading home from supper at the country club. I'd had a bit of difficulty getting baby Jamie into the car seat, which caused Tom to push me out of the way so he could do it properly. This was probably the triggering event. Once we were on our way, he lit into me for chatting with an upstart couple he disapproved of. I was behaving politely to folks who'd greeted me as they were entering and we were exiting. I barely knew them. This was the truth. As you've already guessed, my explanation was futile because Tom was heading for a roll, one that probably had little or nothing to do with the car seat or my friendliness toward the upstarts.

It was an explosion that lasted all the way home. I was interrupted, yelled over, sworn at, and called a liar. All this in front of the kids while Tom drove way above the speed limit. I knew that after I put the kids to bed, I'd have to face the music—and not for the original mistake, but rather for "lying" about it and "starting a fight." It would involve a couple hours of bollocking and the complete destruction of yet another Sunday evening.

How wrong I was. I had to face the music *before* I put the kids to bed.

Tom let us out before putting the car in the garage. I went straight to Jamie's room to change his diaper and put him in his jammies. As I fed Jamie his bottle, I heard Tom throw the car keys down and stomp toward the room. Frothing at the mouth, he smashed the door open. Still sucking on the bottle, Jamie turned his little head to give Daddy a big smile. Daddy ignored Jamie and, instead, proceeded to scream what a fucking bitch I was. I was horrified but said nothing. Daddy then walked right up to me and smacked me hard across the face, knocking the bottle out of Jamie's mouth. Daddy stomped back out, not bothering to pick the bottle up off the floor.

Cradling Jamie, I crawled onto the floor to retrieve the bottle and sat there shaking as I tried to soothe him to sleep. I've no recollection of how I got the other children into bed, but I remember appearing in the living room to receive the remainder of my dressing down.

HAPPY MOTHER'S DAY

One lovely sunny Sunday afternoon, we were finishing off Mother's Day brunch with friends at the club. As we sat in the ballroom used to accommodate the overflow for this event, we vaguely watched the kids outside on the playground and enjoyed a relaxed grown-up chat.

Something set Tom off—perhaps the very occasion. Completely out of nowhere, Tom became angry at me about a request my mother had made at our wedding ten years earlier. She'd asked that we incorporate one of our family's religious customs into the Anglican ceremony. Tom had been incensed by this request at the time but directed his ire at me, not my mother. I made excuses to my mother, who was gracious but no doubt hurt that we were denying her request. I, of course, also had to offer abject apologies to Tom for something I had nothing to do with. I honestly thought that this incident, for which I'd taken it on the chin at the time, was in the distant past.

Though it was out of character at this stage in our relationship, Tom spiraled out of control with anger in a very public setting.

Oblivious to his surroundings, he screamed and swore at me across the table, rehashing the outrageousness of my mother's erstwhile audacity.

Truth be told, my mother's request wasn't so outrageous, with the presiding vicar even welcoming the inclusion of our custom. But Tom needed to be in control, and my mother had waited until the day before the wedding to make her request. Tom wasn't having it, particularly because he felt it was our way of asserting the superiority of our chosen denomination. At the time, I told Tom privately that I was sorry and embarrassed about my mother's gaucheness and asked him to cut her some slack even if he wouldn't grant her request. I reminded him that she was a lady on her own (having been widowed more than a decade before), her hair had just grown back after chemo, and she was on somebody else's turf. She also felt terrible that her health had prevented her from organizing and hosting the wedding herself. Tom ceased and desisted from his wedding eve tirade when his sister reminded us that we all needed to go to bed.

Ten years later at Mother's Day brunch, Tom invoked my mother's vicious, manipulative, un-Christian behavior on the occasion of our wedding. Keeping it as simple as possible, I reiterated how sorry I was about the offense caused and reassured him that we didn't feel superior to him on any score, religious or otherwise, but this fell on deaf ears. Tom was on a roll. Our friends sat there shocked and bewildered. I knew from bitter experience that everything was about to get a whole lot worse.

Sure enough, Tom's shaking, shoulder-raising, and lip-pursing transitioned into a lunge across the table to slap me. Attuned to the finer points of his behavior, I was ready for it. I darted from my chair before he could land the blow. As Tom made his way around the table, I was able flee to a spot behind the ballroom's accordion dividers. From my vantage point, I could see Tom furiously scouring the room for me. When his face was turned, I ran over to the thick ballroom curtains to take refuge in their heavy folds.

I don't know what the waiters who witnessed this were thinking as they watched Tom's mad pursuit, but like the burly fellows at the currency exchange place all those years before, they definitely weren't coming to my aid.

After twenty minutes of hiding, I plucked up the courage to return to the table. I couldn't leave our friends just sitting there, Tom or no Tom. Unfortunately, Tom was already there, and he kicked off again as soon as he saw me. The other husband got up in case he needed to restrain Tom. Our friend then revealed that his father had knocked his mother around during their marriage. He cried at the memory and begged Tom to never strike me again. He also offered to order anger management workbooks for Tom. If only it were so easy. Tom appeared to calm down, and we all pretended to resume a pleasant conversation until it was time to leave.

Of course, once we were in the car driving home, Tom threw the decade-old grievance in my face again. I continued to apologize. Tom was no longer in striking mode, but he had an additional reason to be angry with me, namely that I was the reason he'd gotten so furious in front of our friends.

The promised anger management workbooks arrived but were never opened.

CHESTNUTS ROASTING ON AN OPEN FIRE

A couple more years of normalized nastiness from Tom went by. It was a late Sunday afternoon right before Christmas, and we were enjoying a peaceful moment. The tree was up; the lights had been untangled; the ornaments and garland had been hung. The kids were playing a board game and not yet squabbling. I was heating mince pies in the oven and had even procured Tom's favorite brandy butter to slather on top. What could come in between me and my happiness? Tom and a Sunday shit fit, that's what.

Out of the blue came the rising and falling shoulders, the convulsing body, the quivering face, and the pursing lips I knew so well.

I was scared and privately distraught. A rare hour of serenity was about to be shattered. What the hell was it this time?

Why do you hate my parents so much? Why do you want them to fail? That old chestnut. Well, I didn't hate his parents, who were arriving from the UK later that evening. Moreover, I 100 percent wanted them to succeed because that would mean we could stop bailing them out of their never-ending financial dramas.

While I was blissfully preparing for a nice evening, Tom's thoughts had turned to a conversation we'd had *just a week* before, one that had led to a *mutual* decision based on an unpleasant and costly experience we'd had the last time his parents visited us. On this particular Sunday evening, selectively remembering our recent chat and the ostensibly amicable solution was what provoked Tom's Sunday shit fit.

Two years earlier, when Tom's father and stepmother visited for Christmas, they were constantly on the make. During one very swish Christmas cocktail party, they went to work as middlemen for the inventor of an amazing, earth-shattering, life-changing, planet-saving, next-generation catalytic converter. Grandma and Grandpa Mondo shamelessly fished for financing for the inventor, who hadn't even filed his patent application. All their affluent victims listened politely, but no one took the bait.

At another party during the same visit, my parents-in-law did succeed in striking a deal with the wives of two couples who were friends of ours. Right there at the party, Grandma and Grandpa agreed to be the UK representatives for the ladies' new company, which made train sets, cars, dolls, puzzles, and other wooden toys in an especially impoverished community in a developing country. The ladies were trying to make themselves useful by being social entrepreneurs, and my parents-in-law, to their credit, were trying to make money any way they could.

The first transaction was to be the purchase of the ladies' entire supply of samples by Grandma and Grandpa. I was flabbergasted by this arrangement. Furthermore, it was a racing certainty that my parents-in-law wouldn't succeed in gaining a single order. Playskool and various European brands already had the wooden toy market stitched up, and wooden toys were pretty much out of favor with kids I knew. They already had Buzz Lightyears, American Girl dolls, and early versions of Xbox. And the ladies hadn't bothered getting the wooden toys any child safety certifications. Because of the toys' shoddy construction and questionably sourced, already peeling paint, I was certain they'd never be able to.

Nevertheless, Grandma and Grandpa had big plans to sell these things in Harrods, Peter Jones, and Hamleys. I knew, as did Tom, that the merchandisers of these retailers wouldn't even agree to meet with Grandma and Grandpa. When we got home from the party, I gently explained these insurmountable problems to them, but to no avail. In fact, they were fully expecting *me* to write the check to be handed over to our lady friends the next day, an arrangement Tom had already agreed to behind my back.

I took the chance of arguing with Tom in private because he was in one of his rare "I'm sick of paying their way" modes. However, his manipulative stepmother had worked her evil on him, so this partnership of do-gooders was a fait accompli as far as Tom was concerned. We didn't have a fight, but I was browbeaten by Tom into handing over the equivalent of £800 and driving my parents-in-law forty-five minutes to our friends' place to pick up the stock. I refused to wait for them, though, leaving them to figure out how to lug the boxes back to our place. It was a petty act on my part, but one of the very few times I asserted myself against the parasitical Mondos. Of course, because wooden toys are heavy, we also had to slap our credit card down at the airline counter to pay for Grandma and Grandpa's excess baggage on their return flight home.

Predictably, not a single wooden toy was sold, even at the Saturday market stall my parents-in-law set up when they figured out the enterprise was a dud. I was enraged when, a couple years later, the kids received a wooden train set for Christmas from Grandma and Grandpa—a gift I'd paid for in the first place. I threw the fucking thing in the trash. But I digress.

The waste of our money and my in-laws' time all due to this foolish venture wasn't what bothered me the most. Rather, it was the discomfort, embarrassment, and ill will the fiasco created. Apparently there were some unpleasant exchanges between the parties because the ladies were sorely disappointed that my parents-in-law had failed to set the UK toy market alight with their chipped choo-choo trains. Yes, the ladies were naive, not to mention greedy. However, if Grandma and Grandpa had never become involved with them, Tom and I wouldn't have been tainted by this silly project. The fact that the deal didn't work out soured our relationship with both couples, one of whom we'd known well from another posting. We didn't hold it against them (though maybe we should have), but from then on, whenever we saw them, they were cool toward us, and further invitations we made to them were rebuffed.

It was because of this bitter and humiliating experience two years earlier that I'd mustered the courage in advance of my parents-in-laws' visit to mention my desire to preempt any similar behavior this time around. The timing of the conversation was, for once, not irksome to Tom, and my words were surprisingly well chosen. It was a rare stroke of luck that Tom wholeheartedly shared my view. We agreed that he'd politely but firmly tell Grandma and Grandpa not to approach any of our friends or acquaintances with commercial intent during this visit.

I can only guess that their arrival later that Sunday evening set all the thoughts swirling in Tom's mind, and, as so often happened, Tom rewrote history to make me the villain of the piece. He was unable to acknowledge that he'd completely concurred with me on this topic and had vowed to speak privately with his parents about our nonnegotiable request on the way home from the airport.

Yet, on this Sunday evening, Tom didn't even respond when I asked if he remembered the discussion we'd had less than a week before. You see, the discussion and ensuing agreement didn't fit with Tom's freshly resurrected narrative of "Why do you hate my parents so much?" He had to ignore the inconvenient truth, so easy for him to do when he was in full flow. Fortunately, Tom had to cut short his tirade because he had to leave for the airport to pick up Grandma and Grandpa. At least he abided by our agreement, instructing his father and stepmother not to attempt any dealmaking during this Christmas visit. They appeared to get the message.

CHAPTER 5

HOW TO WIN FRIENDS AND INFLUENCE PEOPLE

FUCKING EUROPEANS

In most social situations and with all sorts of people, Tom could be friendly and charming. He spoke freely, sometimes too freely, to those he felt comfortable with. As mentioned, he also followed my lead when he saw that Nunzia the Connector was succeeding at making others feel welcome and at ease. And he learned to fake bonhomie when he saw it was necessary, although I occasionally had to pay the price for the resentment he felt about having made such herculean efforts with folks he didn't care about.

Fortunately, Tom knew the coded language, humor, and arcane rules of interaction with other English people of his class, which gained us entry to semi-exalted circles in all our postings. When not in a foul mood, Tom appeared to really enjoy their company. Rupert, Henry, Jeremy, Crispin, Charlie, Antony, Jasper, Hugo, and Marcus—along with their wives, Caroline, Henrietta, Tamsin,

Joanna, Victoria, Julia, Clara, Lottie, and Arabella—appeared to return the sentiment. The toffs gave the impression of liking me too; some even deigned to give me their special stamp of approval: "Oh, Nunzia, you're not a typical American." I'd learned years earlier to overlook this "compliment."

I enjoyed their company, though, because they were lively, irreverent, and usually "terribly witty." I forged lasting bonds with some wonderful English ladies, but I'm under no illusions. I must attribute some friendships to the fact that these gals could discuss their unhappiness and insecurities with me because I was trustworthy and, more to the point, outside their inner sanctum. In front of their own, there could never be any chinks in their armor.

This somewhat opportunistic form of friendship didn't bother me because I loved meeting new people of all types and asking them about themselves, which, somehow, I always got away with. Tom admired this quality in me and was happy for me to take the role of social director/collector of friends and acquaintances. Until I was completely ground down in the final years of our marriage, Tom and I had large circles of friends in various locations and active social lives.

But socializing didn't go smoothly when Tom was unable or unwilling to keep his cluster B tendencies in check. The provocation for Tom's descent into party-ruining BPD behavior could be just about anything: someone's inane comment, an opinion unacceptable to Tom, a spurious grudge nursed by Tom, perceived contempt or disregard for Tom, or even someone's nationality. When triggered, he took perverse enjoyment in insulting others (although almost never other English people) with his obnoxious remarks and unassailable opinions. Tom knew better than just about anyone and suffered from no self-doubt on any subject he chose to weigh in on. His favorite subject—the one most worthy of his unbridled contempt—was Europeans.

Dear Reader, you might wonder why I've included the following anecdotes when I wasn't the intended victim of Tom's bad manners.

As you read this section, please try to wrap your head around the anxiety that Tom's unpredictable ugliness toward others caused me. Beyond the anxiety, I experienced genuine grief at the death of friendships I'd cultivated. I still mourn the dear friends and even budding acquaintances I lost because of Tom's malice and shudder when I relive the profound shame I felt during numerous social encounters gone awry.

One of my most abiding embarrassing memories is of a Christmas drinks party in London in the early nineties. That's where twenty-eight-year-old Tom lectured a well-known journalist on the folly of Europe's planned currency union. *Lecture* is the wrong word. Indeed, he *harangued* this gentleman, an Oxford graduate some twenty-five years his senior, on how fucking stupid it was for countries as culturally and economically diverse as Germany, the Netherlands, Italy, and Portugal to enter into a single market, never mind a currency union, when the underlying conditions for such a union weren't fulfilled—and were very unlikely to be in the foreseeable future. The fucking Europeans were morons, and a great democracy like the UK should never cede its sovereignty to fucking unelected bureaucrats in Brussels. Fucking this and fucking that.

On this occasion, Tom knew his stuff, and his tirade was absolutely prescient, but the disrespect and anger he showed this man, who was merely reporting on and analyzing developments, not forming policy, was breathtaking, particularly in a social situation. Tom's arrogance and aggressiveness were physical forces, people repellants. The venerated journalist and bystanders listened politely but removed themselves from the conversation as soon as they could. I was mortified.

After Tom had reaped a few unfortunate professional consequences because of his hubris on this occasion and others, he cottoned on to the necessity of being more circumspect with people he knew to be influential. But, as you'll see, there was no lesson drawn about how he should treat people who had no obvious utility.

AND CHEESE-EATING SURRENDER MONKEYS

During our second posting abroad, we were invited to dinner by Marie-Thérèse and Pierre, lovely French friends from our first posting. All the other guests were French: impeccably dressed, successful, well mannered, and urbane. They were delightful dinner companions, and it all went swimmingly through the champagne and first course. Then, Tom thought it would be a good idea to announce to all assembled that "the French lacked honor." What had prompted Tom to air his long-held pet prejudice in this company? And why could the floor not swallow me up right then and there?

Pierre, who thought he knew Tom well, asked what he meant. *Oh, merde.* I knew what was coming. "Well, the French don't value honesty as we English do... You surrender and collaborate in wars." And the coup de grâce: "You cheat on the rugby pitch."

Tom's words of wisdom cast a pall over the entire dinner party, and the conversation drifted bit by bit into French, effectively excluding us. We were the first to leave.

I never said anything to Tom about his inappropriate remarks because *I* would have become the object of his scorn for the French, thereby ending up the victim of a two-hour bollocking. I wrote a thank-you note to Marie-Thérèse, making reference to Tom's unique sense of humor and hoping privately and completely unrealistically that our hosts hadn't been unduly offended. A couple months later, I was crushed when a mutual acquaintance asked why we weren't at Marie-Thérèse and Pierre's farewell party. I hadn't known they were leaving.

DON'T FORGET THE SCOTTISH GITS!

Not long before our split, when Tom had already descended into full-blown obnoxiousness and derangement, we were invited to dinner by an English couple, excellent hosts who entertained lavishly and skillfully combined their wide circle of friends, acquaintances, and clients. In the midst of guests we were meeting for the first time, Tom contrived a segue in the conversation so that he could tell a Scottish fellow that the Scottish should "just get over it." At the end of the day, any injustice toward the Scottish by the English happened centuries ago! All this was delivered in the most superior, hateful, and derisive tone, with Tom's mouth in what I called "the spiteful smile" and his eyes narrowed in malice.

The Scottish fellow was clearly *apoplectic*, but a swift kick under the table from his wife kept him in check. All he said in response was "I wonder if there are any Irish people at the table who'd like to contribute to this discussion." The host quickly changed the subject, but the other guests continued to exchange shocked glances. I felt so ashamed. Tom didn't. Because the subject had been changed, he felt robbed of complete victory over the Scottish git.

PANDORA'S BOX

One of Tom's few close friends was the very clever Pandora (she of the hollow leg), who'd married in her early twenties. That marriage fell apart; she dated for more than a decade, and most of her boyfriends were very nice. As her fortieth birthday loomed, she went through an unfortunate breakup and moved out of London to rebuild her life and career.

In her new locale, business and love soon blossomed for Pandora. She quickly landed new clients and jumped right into an affair with a married one, Trevor, who claimed his marriage was already dead. For several reasons, though, he wasn't able to get a divorce. This dishonest state of affairs went on for almost five years, during which Pandora received fertility treatments so that they could get pregnant.

It was none of my business how Pandora lived her life, but I let Tom know how horrified I was. Call me old-fashioned, but planning a family with someone who (1) is married to someone else, (2) hasn't yet instituted divorce proceedings, (3) continues to live with his family when he's not on business trips, and (4) spends only the occasional night and dirty weekend with you is both disgraceful and naive. Tom agreed with me but was unwilling to broach this delicate subject with Pandora. This was mainly because she'd convinced him that Trevor was going to get a divorce "any day now."

We met Trevor on several occasions during visits to the UK and found him insufferable, as did our wider social circle, my English friends whom we'd introduced to Pandora. Trevor was bumptious and full of himself, presumptuous and pushy. His sense of humor was crude and unfunny. The icing on the cake: he spoke Estuary![13] How perfectly dreadful! Still, the consensus in our group was that if he made Pandora happy…

However, at a dinner Tom and I hosted in London, this buffoon made it easy for the English folks to cement their low opinion of him. Trevor was on broadcast the entire time and asked no one any questions about themselves. He demanded to see the wine list, weighing in heavily on the wine he'd like to have but would not be paying for. Definitely not PLU.[14]

As an American and just a fly on the wall of the English class system—truly the eighth wonder of the world—I was trying to cut this unfortunate lower-middle-class Englishman some slack. I didn't enjoy Trevor's company but figured he was nervous around us since the other English people at the table were obviously his social superiors, not to mention Pandora's friends, who were no doubt assessing him. Trevor wasn't passing muster. Indeed, his approval rating was slipping by the minute. The particular faux pas that finished him off was his high-decibel, imperious, and completely unnecessary rudeness to the waiter for bringing the wrong vintage, an act performed presumably because he believed the toffs would find it both impressive and amusing. Pretty much

---

13   Estuary, which has its roots in Cockney, is a corrupted form of English spoken by vast numbers of people living in the greater London area and the south of England.

14   *PLU* stands for "People Like Us" and is used by the English upper-middle and upper classes as code for class distinction. This usage predates the adoption of the same acronym by LGBTQIA+ communities.

unforgivable. You see, Tom, Pandora, and our mates, being solidly upper-middle class, would *never* be rude to service staff...in their own country.

About a year after this abject social failure, Trevor finally left his wife to marry Pandora. Tom, in all his wisdom, wrote Pandora an email outlining all the reasons she shouldn't marry Trevor, the foremost being that he was a charmless ass. (Mind you, there was nothing in Tom's screed about the rank dishonesty toward Trevor's wife and family that went on for years.) I told Tom not to press send. Marrying Trevor had been Pandora's dream for years, and it was far too late to mention our objections.

The email was sent and, predictably, never responded to. We weren't invited to the wedding and had no further contact with Pandora. Despite my dismay over Pandora's behavior, I mourned the end of our connection with this clever, original, and welcoming person. She'd been a good friend to me, and I suspect she was the one person who had an inkling of what I had to tolerate from Tom without needing to be told.

The tragic follow-up to this story is that after less than a year of wedded bliss, good ole Trev began treating Pandora cruelly and bizarrely and ultimately left her. After so many failed relationships, the promising new business that never thrived, and years of unsuccessful and soul-destroying IVF, Pandora was bereft and alone, utterly without the hope that was supposed to emerge from the bottom of her mythical box. It was a huge pity that Tom destroyed this relationship because Pandora could have used the love and support of her old friend.

HERE COMES THE BRIDE, BUT LET'S NOT MENTION HER

Tom also eventually destroyed his relationship with his other close friend, Arthur, who married Jocasta. Although Tom detested Jocasta, he agreed to be Arthur's best man.

During his best man's speech, Tom spoke only of his mate

and made absolutely no mention of Jocasta or the bridesmaids! Granted, Tom was young, and it was his first stint as best man. However, he later told me he hadn't planned on saying much about the detestable bride anyway. The fact that she showed up two hours late to her own wedding merely stiffened his resolve.

Happy-go-lucky Arthur seemed not too bothered by this malicious omission on Tom's part, but the same couldn't be said for Jocasta. I thought she needed a semester at charm school but couldn't blame her for her dislike of Tom after his disgraceful performance at her wedding. Some years later, Tom made sure that Arthur, too, knew what he thought of his partner. Although Tom's objections were delivered face-to-face and not as lengthy as the written litany he gave Pandora, this presumptuous act hurt Arthur deeply. As far as I know, he and Tom haven't been in touch again.

CHAPTER 6

DO SWEAT THE SMALL STUFF

IF THE SHOE FITS...

Dear Reader, I'd like you to keep two considerations in mind. First, with a deft abuser, the small upsets almost never remain small. They are like the new layers of snow that slide off a snowpack at the top of the mountain. As they head down the slope gathering up ice, trees, boulders, and more snow, they can become terrible, destructive forces. If she's lucky, the avalanche victim manages to make her way out. By her third or fourth avalanche, she entertains the idea—not completely consciously—that it might be better to stay put.

Second, imagine the constant stress generated by an abuser who *picks, picks, picks* with the goal of instigating an argument or simply devaluing the victim. Even if, by some miracle, no bigger conflict results, she is nevertheless absorbing the impatience, baiting, and nastiness on an almost daily basis. This low-level abuse is often dismissed or excused by abusers as well as relatives, law enforcement, and other observers—sometimes even by victims themselves. But the physical and emotional damage caused by the *drip, drip, drip* of "the small stuff" is incalculable.

After the honeymoon period of my romance with Tom had come to an end, inexplicable upsets over small, very small, *ultra-small* things appeared out of the blue. Initially, I knew on an intellectual level that I'd done nothing wrong. However, as time went on, my confidence and certainty shattered. In isolation, the individual episodes were disconcerting and disorienting, but the accumulation was devastating. The constant confusion made me question and second-guess my hearing, my judgment, and my memory. I became a nervous wreck, always focused on avoiding tiny, inadvertent missteps, posing questions so they couldn't be construed as criticisms, making suggestions so they weren't perceived as challenges to Tom's authority, and desperately trying to unwind clumsy moments of my own creation.

About eighteen months into our relationship, Tom and I took a leisurely Sunday walk on a beautiful London spring afternoon. I wore new Italian loafers made of buttery soft yellow leather. They were comfortable and perfect for strolling. The problem was, Tom wasn't into strolling. He was into power walking everywhere as though we were going to miss something.

We *were* missing something: the glorious spring blooms at Kensington Gardens, which really should demand your attention. We were headed nowhere in particular, and Kensington Gardens was a mutually agreed upon part of the route. So why the hurry?

From the moment we left my place in South Kensington, rushing but occasionally missing the little flashing green man telling us we could cross the road was a constant source of irritation to Tom. Each time we didn't make it, he sighed loudly with annoyance and rebuked me: "What a pity we've just missed this light." Sometimes he crossed without me when I couldn't keep up and then stood on the other side with hands on hips telling me to hurry the fuck up.

It was unrelaxing for me, but I wasn't expecting my relatively slow progress through the park to culminate in a fiasco.

The shit hit the fan when my loafer accidentally fell off my right foot as I stepped onto the curb.

"Why the hell don't you buy shoes that fit?" Tom roared.

Though I was already stressed by the unnecessary rushing and my inability to keep up (but not by Tom's unwillingness to slow down), I was genuinely surprised by the anger and accusation. I scrambled to redeem the situation. "Oh, but they do fit, Tom. I made sure of that. They're really comfortable." I didn't say this firmly or aggressively. I gently tried to communicate that I understood my slowness must be really vexing to him and reassure him that this shoe purchase hadn't been a rash decision.

"How dare you justify yourself when you know perfectly well the shoes don't fit?"

"But, Sweetie, they do fit. One just slipped off as I was trying to keep up with you."

"Don't lie! The shoes don't fit. Don't contradict me. And you walk like a fucking old lady. Get on with it."

On that beautiful spring afternoon, Tom's imperious, thunderous, and outraged pummeling continued all through Kensington Gardens and into Holland Park. Eventually, I became so distressed that I began to cry.

Looking back, I see now that this spring afternoon was a precursor to all the other ruined Sunday evenings that were to come. I wondered then, as I did hundreds of times thereafter, what I'd said wrong or how I could have replied differently to Tom's initial question. Had I been more aggressive or rude than I realized when I answered why the hell my shoes didn't fit? Had my attempt at lightheartedness escalated the situation? Should I have chosen other footwear for the walk?

The episode ended when Tom decided it was time to eat, but his anger and my shame at causing it hovered over the meal.

A COMPLAINT FOR THE AGES

Similar stories played out around minor incidents or nonevents time and time again in our relationship, triggered by Tom's impatience and his conviction that I was answerable to him. His campaigns to devalue me by crushing me into submission were executed masterfully through extreme reactions, arbitrary edicts, and unreasonable deadlines, especially when we had kids. He wanted to catch me out, with the ultimate aim of getting furious with me.

One of Tom's pet peeves was how long it took me to get ready to go out. Over time, I came up with coping tactics to make the getting-ready process smoother, such as laying out my clothes and jewelry the night before an event, having the hairdresser come to the house, putting the hostess gift and the hosts' address and phone number at the front door, making sure Tom understood the event and dress code and reminding him of the other guests' names, and getting the kids and housekeeper organized.

Tom's predeparture bellowing was a habit he cultivated. It was irrelevant that he didn't know whether we had to be somewhere by 7:00 p.m. or 8:00 p.m. It was irrelevant that we were running on time. It was irrelevant that we had a sick child who needed tending to. We had to get out the fucking door by whatever time Tom decreed.

It never occurred to Tom that, in addition to getting my logistically challenged self ready, I took care of all these other necessary tasks, things he took for granted. He never once offered to help with the kids. He didn't bother checking the hosts' address so that he could plan the route to save us time. Instead, he had his butt firmly planted on the sofa watching sports until I finished my frantic effort to get out the fucking door, which, by the way, was sometimes delayed if the match on the telly was too exciting for him to draw himself away from.

During Tom's "Christian years," when he was attempting to be more fair-minded and patient, he asked me a few times how long it would actually take me to get ready. When I responded with a realistic forty-five minutes, he'd get exasperated and demand to know why I couldn't do it faster. Why had he bothered asking if he was going impose his own deadline? Of course, there was no mileage in challenging him on this or in defying him. I'd acquiesce to his "more realistic" demand of half that time. Not only did this lead to incredible stress for me, but, as you've already predicted, I almost never met his imposed deadline, which, in turn, led to more unpleasantness. Tom was setting me up to fail. That was his modus operandi.

DOWN UNDER

Australia is a wonderful country, a favorite destination of mine. My first trip Down Under almost didn't happen, though. It was the midnineties. Tom was on extended gardening leave after switching firms, and he had just spent his Friday afternoon at the travel agent making arrangements for us to travel to Sydney the very next day.[15] So last century, but that's how business was done back then. No online booking of airline tickets, no Airbnb, no Tripadvisor. We had guidebooks and friendly travel agents—that was it. And in this posting, businesses often demanded cash payment.

Tom popped home to show me the itinerary, get his ATM card, and order me to get packing for all of us. But I'd just discovered a serious snag in his plans, thanks to a conversation with a friend who'd returned from Oz the day before. I told Tom I really needed to have a quick word with him before he ran out again. Given that he'd just spent several hours arranging flights and hotels, he wasn't remotely interested in hearing any further input into the itinerary. End of subject.

Tom hurried out to get the transaction done by close of business that day, completely disregarding me. I ran after him and repeated my request to speak with him.

If you've not experienced such an imperious and impatient man,

---

15 Gardening leave is a period during which an employee who has resigned or been terminated continues to get paid but isn't allowed to work for a competing firm.

you won't believe the conversation below actually took place. Some of you, though, will feel the visceral pain of déjà vu when reading my truncated, but verbatim, recounting.

"*Tom!* Really, there is something you need to know before you buy the tickets," I shouted.

"Out with it, then. Stop wasting my time!"

"OK, I've just learned from Jane Smith, who's just come back from Australia, that—"

"Who gives a shit about the Smiths? They travel steerage and hold their cutlery like pens."

Ignoring the ad hominem attack on the Smiths' thriftiness and table manners, I persisted. "*Tom!* Jane told me you have to have a—"

"Spit it out, you stupid woman. I don't have all day!"

"*Tom!* Please don't interrupt anymore because I'm sure you're not aware of this."

"I'm not unaware of anything. I'm the most careful person in the world. I dot my i's and cross my t's, and I have to get the fuck out the door to pay for these bookings."

After to-ing and fro-ing in this incredibly time-eating, demeaning, and unnecessary fashion for almost fifteen minutes, I screamed, "TOM, SHUT THE FUCK UP NOW! WE ALL NEED VISAS FOR AUSTRALIA!"

This salvo of information brought about an immediate cessation of hostilities.

I continued while I had the chance. "The tickets are for tomorrow, and Qantas won't let us on the flight without visas. If we were to somehow get on the flight without visas, the Australians would put us on the next flight out of Sydney, at our own expense. Having been deported, we'd never be allowed back in the country! And the tickets you're about to pay for are nonrefundable. As soon as I hung up with Jane Smith, I called the Australian Embassy to book appointments. We can probably get our visas on Monday and fly on Tuesday, but just to be sensible, I'd suggest changing the reservations to Wednesday."

I was breathless—and astonished—after getting all this out without interruption from Tom.

Tom, with no apology or thanks to me, took his irritation and inserted it along with his tail between his legs and made a quick retreat to the agency to ask if they could please hold off issuing the tickets until Tuesday afternoon.

HOUSTON, WE'VE GOT A PROBLEM

Tom was often on at me about my inability to delegate tasks. On one occasion, I took the chance of asking him to do one teensy-weensy thing for me as he headed to the local emporium to get champagne for our dinner party that evening, booze being his sole responsibility. The neighborhood shops didn't have the chives I needed for the first course. I wouldn't have time to shop for them because I was helping out Louisa's Brownie troop that afternoon, and our housekeeper was fully occupied with preparations at home. I thought Tom could handle chives.

This foray into delegation didn't start, or end, well.

"What the hell do chives look like?"

What! I drew a picture of chives, wrote down C H I V E S and the word for chives in the local language, and then showed Tom a photo of chives in my cookbook so there'd be no confusion whatsoever in his quest to buy this exotic herb. I explained that chives would be in the produce section near the other herbs and that the helpful staff would be able to guide him directly to them.

As Louisa and I headed out to Brownies, Tom was still rattled by this assignment. He barked after me, "You need to tell me exactly what I'm getting and where I'll find it, Nunzia. Is that understood?"

Seriously? What had he done with the precise written instructions I'd given him, and had he even been listening? I was already regretting my decision to send him on this mission.

A couple hours later, as my Brownies were finishing up their sewing, I got a phone call from an agitated Tom, who was standing—completely stymied—in the vegetable section of the emporium.

"Where the fuck are the chives? What do they look like? Where exactly are they? Fucking hell! You aren't thorough enough in your explanations, Nunzia."

I was momentarily dumbstruck but had the presence of mind to move the conversation into the corridor because little ears were picking up the invective coming through the phone. Plus, I had some invective I wanted to send in Tom's direction, namely, "Tom, I didn't ask you to launch the fucking space shuttle. I asked you to please buy *chives*."

As I was about to abort the mission, an emporium employee overheard the brouhaha and accompanied Tom personally to the herb section to find this elusive item.

That was the last time I ever asked Tom to run an errand. His BS was completely deliberate. He wanted to cast me as the incompetent wife and disorganized hostess, and he never wanted to be delegated to again. Tom is a highly intelligent man who has figured out all sorts of conundrums, all far more complicated than locating chives. Like I said, do sweat the small stuff.[16]

---

16 Sweat the Small Stuff trademark registration, United States Patent and Trademark Office, December 29, 2020, https://tsdr.uspto.gov/#caseNumber=88762540&caseSearchType=US_APPLICATION&caseType=DEFAULT&searchType=statusSearch.

CHAPTER 7

CONTROL FREAKERY

NO WORDS...

Tom practiced and perfected a range of abusive habits. One of the pernicious behaviors humming away constantly in the background was Tom's control freakery, which added tremendously to my simmering resentment, accelerated the loss of my self-esteem, and created self-doubt in my abilities, all of which ultimately resulted in my reluctance to make decisions or participate in high-level discussions, even when Tom wasn't involved.

I believe I also experienced alexithymia, which isn't a diagnosis but, rather, an emotional state in which the sufferer cannot express, or possibly even identify, her own emotions.[17] This construct was proposed in 1972 by Harvard psychiatrist Peter Sifneos, who labeled the condition using the Greek words *a*, meaning "lack"; *lexis*, meaning "word"; and *thymos*, meaning

---

17   Imi Lo, "Alexithymia: Do You Know What You Feel?" *Psychology Today*, last updated October 12, 2023, https://www.psychologytoday.com/us/blog/living-emotional-intensity/202102/alexithymia-do-you-know-what-you-feel.

"emotion."[18] Due to the cumulative effect of abuse, I found that words often failed me in high-stress moments with Tom. Especially when things went south at warp speed, I could become profoundly confused, frozen in place, and rendered incapable of getting a response out of my mouth. At times, my alexithymia manifested as unfinished sentences, other times as a stammer. In extreme instances, I recall not being able to say anything at all because I couldn't marshal my thoughts.

Truth be told, I wasn't an adult peer as far as Tom was concerned; I was a recalcitrant adolescent who needed to be grounded and have her privileges revoked. Indeed, on one of the many occasions Tom told me not to contradict him, he also ordered me to go to my room. It should be easy for you to understand, dear Reader, that when a person loses her agency time and again at the hands of a malicious control freak, she could become dysfunctional, temporarily or permanently. In my case, the sense of overwhelm from a recent bollocking sometimes carried over to "peaceful" moments and resulted in me struggling to finish a thought. This would enrage Tom, who'd then scream at me to fucking calm down.

Alexithymia is believed to have a genetic component and can be present in sufferers of Parkinson's, Alzheimer's, MS, and other diseases of the nervous system, including psychiatric illness. It can also result from traumatic brain injury and psychological trauma, including PTSD and complex PTSD (cPTSD).[19] In the absence of linguistic escape valves, the PTSD/cPTSD victim experiencing alexithymia has no way to process or eliminate trauma.

One thing is for sure: decades of living with Tom added up to

---

18   As cited in Peter E. Sifneos et al., "The Phenomenon of 'Alexithymia': Observations in Neurotic and Psychosomatic Patients," *Psychotherapy and Psychosomatics* 28, no. 1–4 (1977): 47–57, https://doi.org/10.1159/000287043.

19   cPTSD can result when a person experiences repeated or prolonged trauma. Sufferers can be sex trafficking victims, domestic abuse victims, refugees, people who are trapped in poverty, and others who deal with physical or emotional hardships on a continuing basis. The *DSM-5* does not distinguish cPTSD from PTSD. However, the World Health Organization includes cPTSD as a diagnosis in the eleventh revision of its International Statistical Classification of Diseases and Related Health Problems (ICD-11).

cPTSD for me, diagnosed when I finally got myself to a psychiatrist in the aftermath of our split. Like many sufferers of cPTSD, I lived with no hope of rescue. The later recognition that my life had been effectively that of a rebellious kid trapped in a brutal military school with no possibility of reprieve confirms (for me, anyway) that my situational alexithymia was a manifestation of deep hopelessness. Until I was given the push I needed, I despaired that I'd be the frequently dumbstruck prisoner of this control freak for the rest of my days.

Tom's need to throw his weight around and assert power over others, especially me—even through ostensibly generous gifts, help, or advice—was a scourge that made my existence a living hell. His need to control all situations, even those that had nothing to do with him, was a symptom of his disorder. Tom would rail against this accusation, but he truly was a relentless, malevolent micromanager.

WHERE IS THE GODDESS OF MERCY?

During Tom's "Christian years," when he was active in men's retreats, he became rather concerned with a number of strictures that I, as a fellow Christian, didn't adhere to. One of my decorating choices in particular made Tom fear for my soul.

Several years earlier, during travels to the Far East, I picked up a carved imitation ivory statue of the Buddhist Goddess of Mercy. Even though one of her hands fell off from time to time, her tall, striking figure held pride of place on my dining room sideboard.

One day, Tom gently approached me to ask if I thought it was right for a Christian lady such as myself to have a Buddhist statue in my home. I was touched that Tom had broached the issue as a question rather than as a command. In fact, I'd been feeling relieved of late that his involvement with these Christian men, whom he respected and appeared to genuinely like, was resulting in his conversion to the idea that men were to treat their wives as treasured partners—as peers with an equal say in family life. Accordingly, I was under the impression that I actually had a choice here.

I replied that the goddess wasn't a problem at all because I didn't worship her. I worshipped only the Christian God of the Holy Trinity. Uncharacteristically, Tom went away quietly. He broached the subject twice more, and each time I reassured him of my Christian faith. The goddess in the dining room was just an objet d'art reflecting a lovely cross-cultural concept. Tom acquiesced, or so I thought.

A week or so after the initial inquisition, I returned to the apartment one afternoon and registered that something was amiss. The Goddess of Mercy was gone! I immediately called for my housekeeper to ask what had happened to the goddess. My housekeeper hung her head, and I knew instantly that Tom was responsible and had instructed her not to tell me what he'd done with the goddess.

I dashed to the back entrance of the apartment, where the rubbish was left. There she was, just waiting for the caretakers to throw her away or take her for themselves. I wiped her down and restored her to her rightful place in the dining room. I mentioned to Tom that evening that I'd found the goddess among the rubbish. He didn't own up to this dirty deed, but then again, he didn't have to because he knew I knew what had gone down. He merely shook his head and sighed. Then he asked me if I was sure I knew what I was doing. It was a ridiculous battle, sure, but one of the few I won.

For what it's worth, Tom doesn't fear for my soul anymore. He's now an atheist and hates me anyway.

PLEASE CANCEL OUR TABLE FOR FOUR

We'd invited the Joneses out to dinner on a Friday evening. Tom was incredibly busy at the office, so I thought I'd relieve him of the task of finding a restaurant and making reservations. I also wanted to show him that I truly appreciated what a super job he did of organizing everything. Restaurants, excursions in the great outdoors, weekend trips, luxury vacations: Tom was fantastic at all of this. The flip side of his impatience was that he went through his to-do list at lightning speed and to a very high standard.

The restaurant scene in our city was booming, so the choice was overwhelming. I called Tom's colleague, the fellow Tom considered the Restaurant Guru and the only person to consult on matters gastronomic. The Guru gave me two hot recommendations, and I was lucky enough to get the last table at one of them. When Tom got home that night, I was excited to tell him what I'd done. He didn't thank me. In fact, he barely replied.

That Friday afternoon, I went to get my hair done. From the hair salon, I emailed Tom to remind him of the restaurant address and reservation time. I also emailed the Joneses to reconfirm.

Tom emailed back that we wouldn't be going to my restaurant because he'd canceled the reservation and made one elsewhere. Confused and hurt, I immediately called him. Despite the many years I'd had to become accustomed to Tom's control freakery, I couldn't quite get my mind around the possibility that he'd gone behind my back just so he could be in control. I thought there must be a good reason for canceling my reservation.

There wasn't. He just didn't like the sound of my restaurant. I was stunned.

"But, but, I consulted your Guru," I stammered.

He ignored that inconvenient truth and simply repeated that he wasn't enamored of my selection.

I then spluttered, "But I've just emailed the Joneses to reconfirm."

Tom flatly replied that he'd already informed the Joneses of the final arrangements and warned me to be on time.

I was crestfallen, not just because my gesture hadn't been appreciated but also because I could no longer pretend away the malice that underlay Tom's many, many acts of control and deception over the years. It was a light bulb moment, an ugly, glaring fluorescent light bulb moment.

Tom's restaurant was empty and charmless, not to mention

hideously expensive. We never went back. A couple months later, we did end up going to my restaurant, thanks to the request of an out-of-town visitor. Tom loved it, and for a time it became our go-to place.

GOING, GOING, GONE

While Tom was snobby and inflexible and harsh in his judgment of others, he and I were united in our aversion to social climbing and anyone putting on airs and graces—something one could never accuse Tom of doing. We spurned the see-and-be-seen set and socialized only with people we liked. Even so, we found ourselves one evening at a very swanky charity gala, where we joined a table hosted by recently socially ambitious friends. I'd rather have gone fishing.

It was an interminable evening. I found the air-kissing and posing of the local great and good and reinvented expats insufferable. I was seated next to a pompous old dignitary who'd donated the burgundy for the event. Therefore, I feigned my enjoyment of the wine, which looked browner and murkier than an old burgundy should and tasted even worse. I kept up my end of the conversation with him and exchanged polite words—and of course air kisses—with the numerous friends and acquaintances who wandered over to pay homage to our exalted table. I couldn't wait to get out of there.

I wouldn't be able to extricate myself, though, until I was forced by Tom to participate in the final fundraiser of the evening. In addition to the silent bidding for unwanted modern art and luxury vacations at patrons' holiday homes, the organizers expected us all to dig deep to support the trained volunteers they sent to foreign parts. I wasn't a fan of this charity and already supported worthy causes personally and through my business.

The midnight auction started with calls for us to fork over one-quarter of the annual upkeep for one volunteer. I sat on my hands while a few tipsy guests on the other side of the ballroom took the bait. The auctioneer got to one-half annual support, and that's when Tom sprang into action, with my company's money. He put on his puppy dog face and a sweet little smile, begging me in front of the rest of the table to *please, please, please have your company sponsor a volunteer*. Absolutely puke-inducing.

For the first few entreaties, I successfully pretended I hadn't heard him. Tom became more insistent, eventually picking up a paddle and putting it in my hand. All this while the folks at our table were sitting on their own hands, pretending not to watch Tom and me. I was mortified and angry. I put the paddle down. Tom maintained the puppy dog face and placed the paddle in my hand again. He then grabbed my forearm and pushed the paddle up into the air.

The quick-witted auctioneer thanked "the lady in the blue Armani gown"—moi—for her generosity, and the entire ballroom applauded wildly with relief. Instantly, a charity official was all over me like a cheap suit to get my signature and contact details. The skinflints at my table were a teensy bit sheepish but no doubt thankful for the distraction.

I was so blindsided and pissed off that I was unable to speak on the way home. Tom realized he'd gone too far, but then again, he had me well trained not to "start fights." I knew well that any objection from me would be met by a host of retorts and ultimately a bollocking. So I just wired the money and stewed. If Tom felt so gung-ho about this charity, he could have easily sponsored a volunteer with his company's money or our personal funds, but this stunt was all about compelling me to do what he wanted.

The following year there was no gala, but there was an email from the charity asking me to renew my support. In the absence of any response from me, the savvy fundraisers approached Tom, who figured out that I was ignoring them. He signed a commitment form *on my behalf*, and I duly received a reminder of their bank instructions. I wired the money.

DESSERT DEBACLE

We often entertained at home before dinner parties became a casualty of the deterioration of our marriage. Tom's escalating cruelty and seething hatred had succeeded in making me feel isolated, worthless, and completely unattractive. Profoundly depressed, I didn't have much will to socialize. I also felt, not completely consciously, that holding a dinner party as a couple was an artifice, a big lie to the outside world that all was hunky-dory in the Mondo household.

I also couldn't muster the considerable effort involved in a dinner party if Tom was going to intervene just for the sake of intervening. There are dozens of examples of Tom's meddling in and disrupting well-planned events.

Tom OK'd the guest lists, selected the wines, and was in charge of decanting and serving them. Otherwise, he didn't participate at all. This was by choice. Remember the chives? Typically, he'd arrive from the gym fifteen minutes before the start of a dinner party, resulting in him greeting guests in a crisply ironed shirt that had become wet from the heat still emanating from his body. Tom wanted to preside. He didn't want to help.

Fortunately, I didn't want or need Tom's help. My housekeeper was an excellent, speedy cook with gorgeous presentation. She and I made a great team and communicated almost telepathically. She and I, along with our regular part-timer, planned everything thoughtfully so that dinner parties were seamless for our guests. Of course, the food and wine were important, but our guests' enjoyment relied mainly on a relaxed atmosphere and leisurely pacing.

After a hiatus of a couple years, Tom asked me to organize a dinner party for sixteen at the apartment we'd recently moved into and lavishly decorated. Perhaps because we were out of practice, the meal itself fizzled. My housekeeper had oversalted the whole lot and had either overcooked or undercooked everything. Some guests barely touched the food on their plates, demolishing the baguettes instead. I was embarrassed but believed we could redeem ourselves with the desserts.

In any case, I could see that the seating plan had been successful. Everyone was having a grand time despite the food! I took the opportunity to nip to the bathroom. When I returned, I intended to head into the kitchen to instruct the ladies to bring the desserts out in twenty minutes.

However, in the five minutes I'd been gone, Tom had gone into the kitchen and instructed the ladies to serve "pudding" (dessert) immediately. They had no choice but to comply with Mr. Mondo's orders.

What greeted me upon my return was the sorrowful sight of the beautiful desserts randomly chucked on the dining table. Tom was doling out the Linzer torte with whipped double cream as though it were cake and ice cream at a five-year-old's birthday. A particularly bossy female guest was hacking away at the gluten-free chocolate ganache cake and plopping pieces on plates that were then unceremoniously passed down the table. Some unwitting victims ended up with two plates of dessert. The dinner plates hadn't even been cleared! *Quelle horreur!*

The guests were unsure how to proceed. Should they start eating what had ended up in front of them, or wait till something more to their liking came their way? Indecision all around. The raspberry pistachio tart and a bowl of homemade vanilla ice cream with a pitcher of Kahlúa on the side stayed put in front of the fellow at the far end of the table. No doubt this poor man was feeling overwhelmed by the plentiful mess before him and lost his ability to think or act. In the absence of a serving knife, someone—somehow—had taken a sliver of the tart. The ice cream just sat there and melted, and the Kahlúa was never poured. The whole thing was a shit show, a dessert debacle.

My housekeeper had been so ruffled by Tom's unilateral orders that she forgot to take the rum semifreddo out of the freezer to soften for a few minutes. Unlike the vanilla ice cream, it was refusing to thaw, so it couldn't be sliced into. Surveying the catastrophe, I concluded that bringing it or the bowl of organic blackberries into the dining room would have just compounded the humiliation well underway.

At this juncture, I'm certain that many of you readers are thinking to yourselves, *Nunzia needs to get a grip. Wrongly served desserts is definitely a first world problem.* So true. But if this is all you're thinking, you've completely missed the point of this little slice of life. Tom knew the ladies and I had things well organized. He knew it wasn't late and that we weren't in a hurry. He knew we had to wait a bit between courses. He knew everyone was having a good time. Given that he himself was participating in an animated conversation, there was no reason whatsoever for him to have left his seat to go into the kitchen to override my instructions—*except to override my instructions.*

It was all about control, and Tom was going to grab any opportunity he could to get one over on me. It was his way of saying, *Nunzia, I'm going to frustrate your plans, major and minor. I'm going to make sure you understand who's in charge. I'm going to let you know that you're incompetent and useless.*

My resentment over Tom's behavior had absolutely nothing to do with bourgeois concerns such as serving dessert properly. This episode went to the heart of the matter: the practical and psychological effects of having all my efforts constantly criticized, overruled, and destroyed.

As with the disposal of the idolatrous Goddess of Mercy and countless other stunts, Tom went behind my back. He went behind my back not just because he wanted to encounter no resistance from me, but also because he needed to exert malicious control.

NO, YOU DON'T WANT THAT

Tom's need to control others developed into a compulsion. His compulsion to control me developed into a sport. We were considering exercise equipment for our recently purchased house on Cape Cod. I wanted an elliptical machine or a treadmill. Tom told me, "No, you don't want either of those." He'd gone on the internet and found something better for me. A rowing machine.

You see, Tom was a mind reader. He was inside my head and knew what I did or did not want. He showed me the rowing machine before ordering it to create the impression that I had input. My physio was adamant that rowing machines weren't for me. More to the point, I hated rowing, but I obviously wasn't going to "start a fight." I zipped my lip. Tom ordered the rowing machine.

Tom nevertheless went to the disingenuous effort of explaining to me that ellipticals and treadmills often break and that rowing machines were better for my cardiovascular fitness.

Not if you don't use them, they're not.

Whatever. I'd already accepted I wasn't going to get what I wanted, even though we could well afford an elliptical, a treadmill, and a rowing machine and had room in our new house for all three. If I'd asked for a rowing machine, Tom would have found a way to say, "No, you don't want that."

In a sort of poetic justice, just a few weeks before we headed to the US to stay in our new house for the first time, Dominic put dear old Dad on the very model of rowing machine he'd ordered. Thanks to Dominic's overzealous workout, Tom wrecked his back. Wrecked as in couldn't move. I had to call in our osteopath to scrape Tom off the gym floor.

The rowing machine was waiting for us when we arrived at Cape Cod. I called a fellow in to assemble it. It was used about four times, and never by Tom. Kind of like that NordicTrack we had in the nineties. At least you can hang your laundry on a NordicTrack.

ONE SET OF RULES FOR TOM, ANOTHER FOR ME

Throughout our marriage, Tom always needed to know where I was. If I was unreachable for even one hour when he wanted to find me, I'd get a proper bollocking later. If I was departing from my usual routine in any way, I was required to give him and our housekeeper my entire itinerary. I had to employ the KISS principle, though, limiting my disclosure to the highlights Tom was capable of absorbing. I cannot tell you, dear Reader, how many times I had to hear "You never told me that." It was either that Tom (1) suffered hearing impairment, (2) had a brain like a sieve, or (3) simply didn't care enough to listen in the first place. I'm going for door number 3.

I admit, I was partly responsible for the bollockings I received when Tom couldn't reach me. Since I'm not an obstetrician, day trader, or secretary of state, I find it rude and unnecessary to have my cell phone out during social or business gatherings. In any event, I always checked my phone frequently and replied to Tom the very moment I saw a communication from him.

I didn't keep track of Tom. After all, he was an adult and could do as he pleased. I now know my grown-up attitude to his whereabouts was completely misguided. The one and only time I asked him where he'd been, he screamed that he didn't need to account to me for his comings and goings. He nevertheless blurted out that he'd been with his colleagues at a party in the countryside. As it turned out, he'd been much closer to home with some rather dubious company.

CHANGING THE GOALPOSTS

Let's turn to an unfortunate and embarrassing example of Tom's inconsistency and unreasonableness when it came to keeping tabs. This may well be the ultimate example of his control freakery.

It happened two and a half years before our split, before I'd reached the realization that Tom hated me. In addition to being genuinely afraid of him, I'd become unconfident, lonely, and physically unwell from the accumulated stress, to the extent that I was virtually a hermit. I soldiered on but with little hope in my heart. Three decades of superhuman efforts, compromises, and love on my part had come to nothing. I wasn't yet aware that Tom was in the grip of dangerous vices, including putting his reliable lineup of sexual partners through training exercises, and that he was discarding me in the process.

On a Friday afternoon in early autumn, Samantha, the daughter of an old friend, arrived for a monthlong stay. I planned to take her to a popular landmark for early evening drinks. Tom and I had communicated by *email* several times that day, so I emailed him to ask if he'd like to join us. I didn't count on it, though, because Friday was often a busy day in the markets. Also, Tom liked to take a gym break (or so I thought) on Friday evenings before returning home.

I emailed Tom again right before 6:00 p.m. but got no response. When Samantha and I left the apartment, it was 6:15. I called Tom, but he didn't pick up. I left a short voice message.

It was a quick ride downtown. As I pointed out the sights to Samantha, I was already feeling anxious that Tom might not have received my email or voice message. I sensed trouble even though, in our communications that day, nothing had augured badly for the evening. In fact, Tom seemed in a jolly mood.

Tom returned my call as Samantha and I were arriving at our destination. He was already furious. "Why the fuck haven't you been in touch?"

What! I'd been in touch by email and phone, and he was, in fact, returning my call. When I meekly pointed this out, Tom ignored that inconvenient truth. Instead, he screamed that I needed to *text* him: texting was the only way to get in touch with him.

Which mode of communication we used was based on the same principle as the disposal of the Goddess of Mercy, the cancelation of the restaurant reservation, the serving of desserts, the vetoing of the elliptical machine. *Whatever Nunzia wants, does, or says, I must thwart her.* In all situations, Tom had to invalidate my words and deeds and assert or arrange for the opposite.

Tom's invalidation skills were well honed: he was the master of extemporaneously changing the goalposts. As soon as I reminded him that I'd emailed, phoned, and left a message that he'd picked up (all this inside of twenty minutes), he came up with texting as the only acceptable way of reaching him. I guess I was too flustered to retort with the most obvious point of all—namely that he could instantly check any sort of communication that came in. He had a smartphone, for goodness' sake!

In addition to being extremely upset, I was embarrassed to death. Tom was screaming so loudly that both Samantha and our driver, who was already acquainted with Tom's foibles, could hear the entire expletive-filled tirade.

As I apologized and promised I'd always text him in the future, Tom continued screaming over me that texting was the way to reach him. I was so shaken by this unexpected turn of events that I tripped as I got out of the car and accidentally hung up on him.

Before I got a chance to ring him back, Tom called again, even more irate because I'd hung up. At that point, I realized he'd been drinking. From the background noise, I could tell he was at a bar near his office. His performance, which would have been heard by his mates as well as other bar patrons, was for public consumption. Mr. Big Stuff was letting his fucking stupid cow of a wife, and everyone else, know who was boss. Impressive.

Tom's extreme meltdown signaled serious ramifications for me. I knew that my punishment had barely begun, and this time there'd really be hell to pay. I hung up again, this time on purpose, without telling Tom where we were. I was genuinely frightened for myself. But the show must go on.

In my agitated state, I did my best to entertain the lovely Samantha, who was now both alarmed and supremely uncomfortable. I asked her lots of questions about herself and gave her some advice about trying to find work in our city, avoiding all talk of myself, Tom, and the kids. At the end of the evening, I took her to the taxi rank. She said, "You're not coming with me, are you?"

Without any explanation from me, Samantha had figured out that I couldn't possibly go home to further abuse. I paid for her taxi back to our place, reassuring her that Tom wouldn't hurt her. I said I'd be home at some point.

I stayed away for almost a week. Tom bombarded me with texts—and, of course, phone calls and emails—with both accusations of malfeasance on my part and promises he'd try to be nicer. He finally lured me back.

It's only now, as I relive this episode, that I realize Tom's need to keep tabs on me was, in fact, completely consistent with his general neglect and disregard for me. It was control freakery, pure and simple, not jealousy or worry that I might go off with someone else.

CHAPTER 8

GASLIGHTING

WHO DIMMED THE LIGHTS?

The term *gaslighting* comes from *Gaslight*, a 1944 film that takes place in Victorian London. It's based on an earlier film and play of the same name. The baddie, who wants to find loot his wife has inherited, systematically attempts to destroy her sanity by taking things and planting them elsewhere and by dimming the gaslight and then denying to her that any of this has happened. Bit by bit, the wife comes to doubt all her perceptions and, ultimately, her sanity. She prevails in the end, though.

In her excellent book *The Emotionally Abusive Relationship*, Beverly Engel says a gaslighter will deny that particular events took place or that he said something you both know he said as a means of discrediting you and/or as a way of justifying his abusive behavior.[20] According to Dr. Engel, gaslighting is both "conscious and deliberate." I can't be sure which of Tom's thousands of individual

---

[20] Beverly Engel, *The Emotionally Abusive Relationship* (John Wiley & Sons, 2023).

acts of gaslighting were conscious and deliberate, but I recognize that some were psychologically necessary for him.

Let's consider Tom's denial of the South American airport incident recounted in Chapter 1. I believe he had to rewrite history for his own sake. As he matured and his career progressed, he couldn't cope with the shamefulness of his behavior as a twenty-nine-year-old. He must have realized this incident reflected badly on him, so all traces of it had to disappear. Tom didn't say to me, "We can't talk about this any longer." He said, "It didn't happen." I honestly don't know if the denial of this story, one he'd told so many times, was conscious and deliberate.

For me, it doesn't matter whether the gaslighting is conscious and deliberate or not. It's an insidious and incredibly damaging form of abuse. When you've been gaslighted by an expert gaslighter, you don't know what's just hit you. You're so flustered and disoriented that it's almost impossible to remember the sequence of events or the conversation—to the extent that you're unable to sort them out for yourself afterward, much less recount them to someone else. Tom frequently executed gaslighting through aggressive rapid-fire questioning that gave me no time to answer and allowed him to dictate the outcome of the one-way battering. Other times, Tom's gaslighting was of a more mundane variety. He'd just mess with my head by denying what was true or asserting what obviously wasn't.

CLEAN OUT YOUR EARS!

By the time we'd been at our second posting a few months, Tom succeeded in convincing me that I had a hearing problem. He'd claim he'd said things I hadn't heard at all or tell me my hearing was bad when I hadn't understood something he'd said. "You need to clean out your ears, Nunzia, and listen more carefully!" Still a young woman, I became increasingly worried about my hearing deficit.

One Friday afternoon, after an especially unpleasant clean-out-your-ears phone call with Tom, I was positively panicked. I called the hearing center on the other side of town. It was already closing time. I begged them to stay open and sped there in a taxi.

After a battery of tests, the technician informed me there was nothing wrong with my hearing. I said that couldn't be so. I insisted on another round with a different technician in the other testing room; I'd pay for two sets of tests. They complied and kept the clinic open until the second exam was completed. Again, they found nothing wrong with my hearing.

That night, I told Tom the results. He dropped the subject of my poor hearing for a few years but resurrected it when the kids were old enough to get in on the joke. The children have subsequently admitted to me that they mumbled on purpose. Whenever I asked them to repeat what they'd just said, they'd aggressively shriek the same words in my face. This is an especially painful memory for me.

Even our youngest, Jamie, remembers the year Tom ordered me a hearing aid from the classified ads for Christmas. This medical device was presented as a serious gift, a token of Tom's genuine concern for me. What Tom really wanted was to have a laugh at my expense, cause me massive insecurity, and belittle me in the eyes of our children. Tom succeeded on all counts and gradually built upon the doubt he sowed about my hearing to intimate that Mummy shouldn't be taken seriously.

In the final years of our marriage, Tom almost convinced me on a few occasions that he'd not said something I was certain I'd heard him say. Once he told me I must have *dreamed* it, leaving me genuinely bewildered. To amplify the effect of his gaslighting, he told me I was *damaged goods, an old lady, a millstone around his neck*. Because Tom had already annihilated me, these insults had very little effect on my emotional state. However, they did make me think I needed to consider the possibility that I was experiencing cognitive decline associated with early onset dementia. I couldn't bring myself to investigate this further, though, because all my energy was reserved for just making it through the day. The awful possibility of dementia, along with other desperate worries, sank to the bottom of my emotional morass, where it lingered and discomfited me, never fully processed or accepted.

Tom did his utmost but, fortunately, never completed the job of convincing me I was suffering from hearing loss, dementia, or other serious cognitive deficits. As Tom began to truly unravel toward the end of our relationship, he did and said things that let me know for sure that he was gaslighting me—and that *he* was possibly losing *his* marbles. This realization was cold comfort, though, because I was too physically and emotionally weak to put the situation to rights.

Despite my lack of understanding surrounding the motivations behind Tom's crazymaking behavior, perhaps I should at least consider Dr. Engel's assertion that gaslighting is a conscious and deliberate act. Specifically, how can an otherwise functional person completely blot out what he said just weeks, or even moments, before? Perhaps Tom's behavior in the following two anecdotes was conscious and deliberate, the product of a malicious and well-honed compulsion.

I HATE YOUR SISTERS AND NEVER WANT TO SEE THEM AGAIN

Several months before the texting misstep I described in Chapter 7, Charlene, our Christian marriage counselor, came to town and offered us a face-to-face session. We readily accepted, but for different reasons, as you'll soon see.

As Tom and I sat on the terrace, waiting for Charlene to arrive, he told me out of the blue that I wasn't to blame for the rift with my sisters. He added that I'd always treated them kindly and generously. I'd remained good to them even in the face of their bad behavior during the final months of my mother's life and the subsequent winding up of her estate. He ended this unexpected compliment with "I hate your sisters and never want to see them again." Verbatim.

What adult uses the word *hate* to describe his feelings toward other people? I didn't hate my sisters, and if only you knew what I'd put up with from Tom's family... I should have sensed that Tom's extreme sentiment didn't bode well for our session with Charlene.

As soon as we got started with Charlene, Tom was off and running, saying that I always started arguments with people: with him, my children, my housekeeper, my employees, and *my sisters*.

I was surprised to learn about my universally argumentative nature and beyond incredulous to hear that my sisters were victims of my alleged belligerence! When I finally got the chance to speak, I said, "But Tom, just five minutes ago you told me how wonderful I'd been to my sisters, how beastly they'd been to me, and how I'd overlooked their spitefulness and jealousy."

Charlene said, "Is that true, Tom?" On this occasion, perhaps because the change of story had been caught so early, Tom had to admit that, yes, it was true he'd said that.

BUSTED!

This was a Pyrrhic victory, however. Charlene got the session back on track, but ten minutes later Tom stood up, gesticulating and yelling at the top of his lungs. He told Charlene she was fired and to get the fuck out of his house. Clearly, Charlene hadn't gotten the session back on track. Not only had Tom been caught gaslighting, but, faced with Charlene's calm but pointed questioning, he was also being frustrated in his objective of painting me as the problem in the relationship.

Charlene got up to leave, quiet and compliant. Embarrassed by his outburst, Tom begged her to stay. We finished the session and then took her to dinner as though nothing untoward had happened. For weeks thereafter, Tom was still put out by the contretemps. He soon stopped having phone sessions with Charlene, citing lack of progress over the significant amount of time we'd spent with her.

I could understand Tom's increasing unwillingness. We had indeed made little progress with Charlene, and her sessions were expensive. Every step forward seemed to be followed by two steps backward thanks to the resentment her approach elicited in Tom. (Her profoundly sexist and faulty Bible Belt guidance on marriage was almost beside the point.)

Another important contributor to the demise of the counseling relationship with Charlene was Tom's newfound atheism, brought on by the belief that his prayers had always gone unanswered. A spate of recently published atheism books, such as *God Is Not Great* by Christopher Hitchens and *The God Delusion* by Richard Dawkins, reinforced Tom's certainty that God did not exist. In fact, he admonished me to drop my faith as well. "You'd think you'd believe your husband, Nunzia. I've done research into this. God doesn't exist." You cannot make this up.

Tom told me I could continue with Charlene if I wanted to. I did, but both she and I agreed after a few more sessions that it was fruitless without Tom's ongoing involvement. I informed him we wouldn't have to wire her any more money because I'd decided to end the sessions. Tom said, "Good, because Charlene is a fucking moron. I hate her." Verbatim.

DON'T BE SO NON-U, NUNZIA

The following incident could easily go under the heading of Control Freakery alongside the dessert debacle. However, I think it best belongs here because, like the quick change of story in front of Charlene, it was helpful in showing me that I was neither hard of hearing nor losing my faculties. The problem, and a very alarming one at that, was Tom's.

This meltdown, occurring not long after the dessert debacle dinner, is an illuminating example of two abusive habits Tom used in concert: (1) causing extreme chaos and (2) gaslighting in the form of pretending that he never said what he definitely did say.

Regarding the former, Tom wanted to exert malicious control to throw me off balance right before a dinner party, a massive upset the entire household had come to expect. Regarding the latter, it is virtually impossible that Tom forgot one of his recent decrees. Instead, he was providing further evidence that he needed to cause pandemonium and was pathologically forced to dissemble to accomplish this. (As with the South American airport incident, it occurs to me that Tom's gaslighting might have been conscious and involuntary rather than conscious and deliberate.)

Our inventory of handblown champagne flutes had dwindled, the glasses having been chipped, cracked, or broken by careless clinking or washing over the years, and two had been smashed at the last dinner. I let Tom know I was about to make an online order in hopes of having replacements delivered before an upcoming client dinner. Tom always expected me to have the household running smoothly, so I anticipated at least a grunt of approval from him. To my great astonishment, I was sharply chastised. "Don't be so non-U, Nunzia.[21] You don't need matching champagne glasses. We can use the others we have round the place. Don't waste the money."

That was a first from Tom. He was never concerned about money and certainly didn't think splashing out on beautiful things was a waste. And he often bragged that he was the spender in the family, not me.

Whatever. I complied. I didn't order the champagne flutes.

Fast-forward to the evening of the client dinner. Tom was carrying out his dinner party booze duties, which included putting the champagne on ice and setting the champagne glasses on the tray. For no good reason, I was in an optimistic, happy frame of mind. My florist had outdone himself on the table arrangements, the candles were lit, the food was going to be luscious, and the guests were a fun, interesting group. I was finishing my eye makeup in this

---

21 *Non-U* means not done by the upper-middle/upper classes in Britain.

breezy mood when I heard screaming all the way from the kitchen. I ran there with my heart in my mouth, thinking that someone had been seriously injured. Tom was standing in the doorway, holding a champagne flute and shrieking at the housekeeper and part-timer.

When I appeared, he turned his wrath on me. "Why the hell is there not a full set of champagne glasses? Why did you not check that you had a full set if you were having a dinner party? Who has a dinner party without a full set of champagne glasses? You are fucking incompetent and unreliable, Nunzia."

My jaw dropped. My housekeeper and I looked at each other in utter bewilderment. She'd been there when I was ticked off for being so non-U as to want to replace chipped and broken champagne flutes.

I waited till Tom paused for breath before reminding him that he'd instructed me specifically not to order more glasses. *Have you forgotten that?* I pleaded. *It was a little over three weeks ago!* He heard me but resumed his fulminating. He wasn't listening, possibly because he couldn't cope with the undeniability of his changed stance or the embarrassment of having been busted.

Whatever the case, Tom was hell-bent on causing mayhem. His shrieking didn't completely subside until the doorbell rang, announcing the arrival of the first guests. I wonder if they heard any of Tom's tirade. I wonder if I was able to recover my composure fast enough. I wonder if any gossip circulated about the goings-on chez Mondo. After all, most neighbors had been treated to our noisy "discussions," and over the years a few were bold enough to drop disapproving hints. It's entirely possible that our volatile relationship was the talk of the town without us ever knowing.

There is only one thing I'm certain of: Tom's unpredictable eruptions, made so much more potent by his deft gaslighting, left me an anxious wreck. This time around, though, at least I knew I wasn't crazy or hearing-impaired because my housekeeper was able to tell me so.

CHAPTER 9

FAST DRIVING: AN ADDICTION AND A FORM OF ABUSE

THE NEED FOR SPEED

Driving fast not only made Tom feel invincible; it was also a way of tyrannizing me, giving him a sense of power that filled a psychic hole or two. Just to be clear, though, Tom's fast driving wasn't just for causing me supreme discomfort; it was to subdue and impress others and to frighten the shit out of them for a good laugh. Many grown men will no longer get into a car driven by Tom, and many families over the years made their own transportation arrangements when they heard that Tom was taking the kids to rugby, ice skating, or a birthday party. Tom's driving misdeeds are legion. I'm spoiled by choice when selecting what to recount to you.

Driving was an extension of Tom's manhood. Even as a new driver, he liked other motorists to know what he was made of. Legend has it that when Tom was eighteen, he got into a drag race with a Rolls-Royce around Grosvenor Square, former site of the American Embassy in London. After a couple of loops around the square, it went pear-shaped for both drivers when they collided in front of the embassy. Both cars were totaled, but, miraculously, the drivers walked away unscathed. The problem emerged only later when his father realized that Tom hadn't been put on the insurance. Dad allegedly figured out a way of getting Tom onto the policy "retroactively."

Crashes, prangs, and near hits aside, it must be said that Tom was a skilled driver. During a lesson at one of Britain's Grand Prix raceways, the rather irritated instructor told Tom he had nothing to teach him. Off the raceway, Tom also enjoyed showcasing his talents. He was compelled to challenge Porsches and Maseratis in our family car with the kids and me inside. In fact, because of his chutzpah, determination, and incredible hand-eye coordination, he'd often win with our tank of an SUV, leaving the Porsches and Maseratis in the dust and their drivers aggrieved. In his sports cars, he always won the drag races.

ROAD RAGE, BEFORE IT WAS A THING

Tom cut people up and often flustered less skilled but perfectly adequate drivers attempting to get from point A to point B in a safe manner. We have the distinction of having been chucked the finger on four continents and were probably the first perpetrators of "road rage" in Britain.

On an otherwise peaceful Saturday afternoon in London, Tom darted in front of another vehicle. This was a completely unnecessary maneuver because traffic was slow and heavy, and we weren't going to make the green light. When we got to the intersection, the other driver screeched to a halt, jumped out, and accosted us. The fellow was incensed, ready to punch Tom's lights out. Tom, the smaller of the two gentlemen, wasn't cowed and sprang out of our sexy, nippy Saab Turbo to engage in the confrontation.

"I don't think you want to be seen socking me at this busy junction, mate," Tom taunted. Tom's point was well taken. Effing and blinding ensued, but no blows were exchanged.

After several minutes of screaming and honking from the cars behind us, the fellow's wife and I hopped out and managed to get our idiots back into their respective cars so we could all continue on our way.

NO, OSSIFER, I HAVEN'T BEEN DRINKING

Tom truly enjoyed the driving experience, especially on the Autobahn and any open road where he could get away with flooring it. As a frequent passenger, I came to realize that driving was also an outlet for Tom's deep-seated anger—an anger that was sometimes fueled, but not caused, by alcohol. Moreover, driving was one of the many realms in which Tom could show that rules were for other people. This included not only speed limits but also the prohibition on drinking and driving.

Early in his career, Tom drove a London colleague home from a boozy dinner, one of dozens they shared. The police stopped Tom for speeding and intended to Breathalyze him. Fortunately for Tom, they'd inadvertently left the Breathalyzer back at the station. This close brush with the law really should have put the wind up Tom, but as with his arrest for assault, he barely felt its impact.

Tom went on to drive while over the limit many more times. I occasionally succeeded in getting him to leave the car where it was, to be picked up the next day. However, when he wasn't persuaded, I was too gutless to grab the keys from him or refuse to get in the car. The possibility of physical retribution was too high. I shudder to think of the devastation my path of least resistance could have wreaked.

RECKLESS, ME?

In one posting, we were driving at speed up a major artery. Tom quickly changed lanes before the road became a single carriageway. Most drivers wouldn't have considered such a stunt, but Tom easily pulled it off. I didn't react because I was used to his driving and not especially alarmed. Plus, if you haven't already figured it out, it wouldn't have been worth my while to call attention to it, even with a gasp.

The driver Tom cut off wasn't as chill as I was. As a matter of fact, he was enraged, probably because he saw his life flashing in front of him as we appeared out of nowhere and whipped right in front of him. Somehow, in the blur that was us, the disgruntled motorist caught and jotted down our license plate number. The next day, he wrote to the DMV to complain about Tom's driving.

Tom was issued with a summons but chose not to defend himself. He was offended, though, that he'd been charged with reckless driving. He wasn't reckless at all. How could anyone as skilled as he be branded reckless? He pleaded guilty and accepted the points off his license.

BOY, STEP OUT OF THE VEE HICK EL WITH YOUR HANDS UP

A few years after that legal run-in, we hosted a vacation for our extended families in Florida. Tom left the house later than he should have to pick up various unaccompanied kids flying into Orlando. He therefore sped in our mammoth rented Caddy all the way, blissfully unaware that for at least part of his dash he was being tailed by a Florida state trooper. The state trooper, who allegedly chased Tom for more than five miles with his sirens blaring, was beside himself with fury when he finally caught up with him. Tom told me he'd been doing twice the speed limit. Two of our own kids were in the back seat.

Because the good folks of Osceola County were completely

thrown by a British driving license at that time, Tom was let go. He was, however, required to show up a week later at the courthouse to pay a fine of several hundred dollars. Due to the delay "caused by the state trooper," Tom ended up truly late to pick up the arriving kids. It was just dumb luck that he found them wandering, tearful and distressed, through the bustling airport.

It should be noted that if Tom were caught going twice the speed limit in the UK, he'd be charged with dangerous driving and almost certainly sent directly to jail. Conviction would carry a maximum prison sentence of two years, an unlimited fine, and permanent disqualification from driving.

THANKS FOR LUNCH!

One Saturday afternoon in our final home base, Tom insisted we drive a friend to his next appointment. After lunch, we piled into the car, and Tom sped down a narrow road where numerous heedless people were taking weekend hikes. I thought to myself that a tiny miscalculation on Tom's part, or the hikers', could end in disaster. And I saw that our friend was petrified.

I made the rash decision to ask Tom to slow down, but he simply turned up the thumping Jamiroquai and stepped on the gas. Once we'd accelerated through the pack of ramblers with a few honks of the horn, Tom raced to our destination, negotiating every turn with exaggerated steering to achieve maximum fear and car sickness. He was laughing the whole while.

When Tom and I split, this friend told me that as soon as we dropped him off and sped away, he stumbled a few steps and threw up his lunch. He, along with other friends, informed me that they knew Tom was cruel to me and inconsiderate of others—and that he took needless risks while driving, risks that could have easily resulted in death.

LASTING TRAUMA

I could regale you with countless other traumatic driving incidents featuring Tom as driver or passenger. However, I'll end this chapter with four more that best illuminate Tom's unreasonable behavior and explain its serious lasting consequences for me and our children.

There was Tom's blazing row with his sister Camilla on the M4, the motorway that goes from London to the west of England. I sat in the back seat with baby Dominic while Tom raged at Camilla, his body in furious spasms as he swerved from lane to lane at 110 miles per hour. I really thought we were finished. Unsurprisingly, I still get flashbacks of this terrifying experience. What caused Tom's meltdown? Camilla's request that he abide by the speed limit.

There was the time I did my first long motorway drive after earning my British driving license. Tom thought it would be a good idea to scream at me about my driving technique as we reentered the outskirts of London. I was so worn out from the concentration required for that maiden voyage of several hours and flustered by his ranting and raving that I pulled off the road on a major roundabout, got out, and told Tom to drive. There was no opportunity for him to argue with me as we literally hung off the side of the roundabout with heavy traffic behind us.

There was the time Tom pulled a similar stunt in our first posting abroad. I was again on my maiden voyage in a new country, and he was again screaming, but this time not bothering to specify what I was doing wrong. I asked, but he only continued to shriek my name repeatedly. I looked in the rearview and side mirrors and saw nothing alarming. I was driving the same speed as everyone else on the busy road, and the light was still green. As Tom continued to shriek but not clarify, I panicked.

Assuming I was about to run somebody over, all I could think to do was apply the brake. When I did that, the motorcyclist who was already driving up my ass (as bikers seem to do all across the world), smashed into the back of our car. He was fine, but his bike was totaled. We spent the next three hours in the police station, drawing diagrams and explaining our respective versions of the accident. (Tom's shrieking, as it turned out, had stemmed from his opinion that I was driving too close to the concrete roadwork barriers on the passenger side of the car.)

The police deemed the motorcyclist at fault, which was a relief. However, being shrieked at by Tom while driving, causing an accident my first time out, and ending up in the police station with an interpreter called in to assist with my interrogation was all too much for me. I didn't drive for two years after that, until the necessity of transporting two small children in proper car seats forced me to give it another go.

Fifteen years thereafter, in another posting, I was returning from a weekend hike when I witnessed the spectacular crash caused by a harried and impatient Tom as he turned out of our driveway without looking both ways. The oncoming car he hit spun around three times, causing a dent to our bumper but a complete write-off of the other car. The driver was stunned but fine. Tom commented to me that "It was jolly lucky no hikers were walking on the other side of the road because they would have been thrown up in the air and then down the mountain, never to be seen again." Perhaps he meant those words as comfort, but I was shaken to the core by them. All these years later, I still experience visions of an innocent hiker flying through the air to their death on a beautiful Saturday morning.

In a nutshell, the trauma Tom inflicted as driver or passenger while in a moving vehicle has caused me deep anxiety around driving. His god-awful behavior has gone far beyond contributing generously to my cPTSD. It's had a practical consequence. I refuse to get behind a steering wheel anywhere in the world because I'm scared rigid that I'll kill or injure someone. The gig economy innovations of Uber and Lyft came just in time for me.

While well-documented dangerous driving incidents featured in the affidavits for our divorce trial, my lawyers were unsuccessful in getting the judge to consider them as part and parcel of the abuse I suffered. Indeed, the judge ultimately decided she wasn't interested in adjudicating a case involving abuse of any type, and I was forced to withdraw this claim. Unfortunately, as a mere public safety issue, Tom's driving was outside the purview of family court.

As I end this chapter, I should tell you that none of our children, two in their twenties and one in his thirties, has a driver's license or any plans to get one. You can well imagine that sitting in the back seat during so many hair-raising rides, witnessing Daddy get pulled over by a furious Florida state trooper as well as cops elsewhere in the world, and being in the car for the spectacular mountainside accident would put them off driving forever. The kids are fully aware that cars are lethal weapons and that one mistake, reckless or not, has the capacity to ruin many lives.

CHAPTER 10

DEFINITELY DISGUSTING

THE TWILIGHT ZONE

Even before Tom's descent into unfettered porn consumption, wide-ranging adultery, and all-around degeneracy, he did some pretty disgusting things, many of which still haunt me. To name a few, there was the affair he had when I took baby Dominic to meet my family in the US. Then there was the time he got crabs, transmitted them to me, and blamed them on the "filthy linens" at the five-star resort we'd been at the week before. (He eventually came clean on that one some years later after returning from a Christian men's retreat.) And how could I forget the time he sheepishly called from work to ask if I'd take the wedding ring out of his trouser pocket before the suit was collected by the dry cleaners? He'd been at a girly club the night before and apparently felt embarrassed to be wearing a wedding ring. Seriously? Embarrassed in front of escorts and strippers? Isn't it their job to entertain married men?

If you're not shocked or repulsed yet, you will be by his antics during our final three years together.

At the beginning of Tom's downward spiral, he had a minor medical issue that required a day procedure. He decided on a pain minimization/sedation technique known as monitored anesthesia care (MAC), or "twilight," whereby you shouldn't feel pain from the procedure but come out of your stupor faster.

On the morning of the surgery, I accompanied Tom to the hospital and sat in the waiting room. Before noon, the surgeon came out to tell me the problems he'd detected and remedied were minor, the procedure had gone well, and I could take Tom home shortly. I slipped into Tom's curtained-off cubicle for a brief, reassuring chat. I told him I'd reappear in twenty minutes to help him get dressed. As I walked back into the waiting room, I heard buzzers and bells go off and saw nurses and doctors run into the recovery room. I thought, *Uh oh, somebody's day case didn't go so well* and said a little prayer for them.

Exactly twenty minutes later, I went in to get Tom dressed and packed up. His bed was surrounded by medics of various types. The surgeon turned to me and said, "The problem was that—"

What problem?

Turns out those buzzers and bells had been for Tom. As soon as I walked away, his blood pressure plummeted dangerously. The medical team kept him in the hospital for observation for two nights. They were concerned that there was something wrong with Tom's heart.

We were both rattled, and I didn't leave Tom's side. The surgeon ordered more tests but could find nothing. Tom would have to go through another set of outpatient cardiology exams the following week. When the hospital released him, I took him home and deposited him directly in bed.

Tom's condition was a roller-coaster for the first week, with the first three days at home very frightening. He was weak and pale and couldn't get out of bed on his own. He groaned constantly and complained frequently of nausea and dizziness.

On day two at home, there was a moment when Tom believed

he was about to die. Gravely and deliberately, he delivered a drawn-out "Nunzia, I'm sorry," but didn't elaborate. I told him I was calling an ambulance. The spinning and nausea passed after a couple of minutes, and he said no, he wasn't going back to any hospital or to fucking doctors who didn't know what they were doing.

On day three at home, Tom was still weak and bedridden but able sit up to use his computer for a few minutes at a time. He Googled *twilight anesthesia* and became increasingly morally outraged by the hour. The rabbit hole Tom had burrowed himself into led him to the not-very-objective conclusion that twilight anesthesia is dangerous, full stop.

My research and follow-up conversations with specialists produced another conclusion altogether: that twilight anesthesia is perfectly safe for the vast majority of us when administered by a qualified and experienced practitioner. Dear Reader, Tom's rush to judgment highlights two pitfalls we should all avoid: (1) reliance on online medical research and (2) confirmation bias, especially when fueled by fury and indignation.

Tom's follow-up visit to the cardiologist didn't help. He felt that she was barking up the wrong tree with her various tests. Tom sharply rebuked me when I suggested that he cooperate, given that he'd always worried about his heart—and given that his reaction to the anesthesia was so unexpected and severe. At the very least, we'd be able to ascertain that he should never be put under twilight anesthesia again. At the end of a week at home, Tom was still hostile and grumpy but, mercifully, well enough to go back to work.

After two weeks of fulmination about the incompetent medical profession, Tom's ranting and raving abruptly ended, and he'd no longer engage in conversation about his medical travails. I was worried and wanted answers to the extent they were possible. My opinion didn't matter, though. In fact, my insistence that we uncover the cause of this serious incident was rather vexing to Tom, who'd complained over the years that I didn't care about his health. (He'd even accused me on occasion of wanting to kill him.)

So my search for the truth was unilaterally and inexplicably shut down. There was, however, a likely answer to this medical mystery, one that Tom possibly realized for himself but didn't want to divulge to me. I wonder if you're thinking what I'm thinking. Hint: this procedure happened when Tom had been displaying a poor appetite at home and his away games had become more frequent.
Well?

Bingo! Sildenafil, also known by the brand name Viagra, reduces your blood pressure. If I were a betting person, I'd say Tom was using sildenafil and hadn't disclosed that fact to the anesthesiologist, probably because he thought its effects were so short-lived that disclosure wouldn't be necessary.[22] Apparently, it is possible for the active ingredient in these erectile dysfunction drugs to stay in the system for more than the widely assumed twenty-four hours. In fact, the National Institutes of Health (NIH) recommends that a patient stop taking sildenafil one week before surgery.[23] Sildenafil, which causes the release of nitric oxide, might interact with the anesthesia to result in dangerously low blood pressure, leading to adverse consequences. The NIH has received reports of several cases of permanent blindness, even when this drug was ingested thirty-six hours before anesthesia was administered.

I must confess that I didn't get to the odds-on bottom of this medical mystery until I was able to return to our marital home after finally getting Tom to leave. First, I found an empty packet of Viagra resting at the top of the pile in the trash can in our bedroom. Second, at the time of this distressing medical episode, I'd seen a piece of paper with puzzling notes in Tom's handwriting, which, to keep the peace, I didn't ask about. In light of the salvaged Viagra packet, the terminology on the note now made some sense. My discovery also led me to think again about the abrupt end to Tom's

---

[22] All of us should know that ahead of any medical procedure, or even when being prescribed a new medication, we must disclose all drugs, legal or illegal, and any herbs or supplements we've recently used.

[23] V. Fodale et al., "Viagra, Surgery and Anesthesia: A Dangerous Cocktail with a Risk of Blindness," *Medical Hypotheses* 68, no. 4 (2007): 880–882, https://doi.org/10.1016/j.mehy.2006.08.031.

tirade about the corrupt and incompetent medical profession and why he was unwilling to go forward with further investigation or possible legal action when an anesthesiologist acquaintance of ours offered us free help in reviewing his case. The refusal of this generous offer truly puzzled me at the time.

During the financial disclosure stage of our divorce, I then figured out why Tom had said, "I'm sorry, Nunzia" when he believed the end was nigh. He wasn't apologizing for the inconvenience of me needing to watch and worry over him or for the heartbreak of my imminent widowhood. No, he was apologizing for all the activity I'd unearth when I looked through his credit card and bank statements as I was settling his estate.

A WALK-ON PART FOR NUNZIA IN TOM'S BRAZEN DUPLICITY

This episode demonstrates just how bold, deceitful, and gross Tom had become. It happened just weeks before our split, when Tom had become adept at lying and I had become a basket case, unable and unwilling to see things that were directly in front of me.

Tom had just returned from several weeks on the road, a "marketing trip" that I later found out was not only unnecessary but also probably instrumental in the downfall of his business.

Without explanation, Tom commanded me to make a dermatologist appointment for him, which I promptly did. He brought home oral and topical antibiotics from the doctor. I was required to rub cream on the rash covering his back and shoulders.

Under the bright bathroom lights, I searched for the rash but could see nothing. I asked Tom to direct me to the right spots. He snapped that there was a rash and to just get on with it. I squeezed out the cream from the tiny tube and did as thorough a job as possible under the circumstances. I handed him back the tube and noticed that he then slapped some cream elsewhere. For my own safety and sanity, I had to pretend that sight away.

The drill was the same for the next two mornings. On day four, he didn't ask me to rub the cream on his back and shoulders, so I asked if I should do that for him. "Oh, yeah, yeah" was his flustered reply. I recorded but didn't process this behavior. At the end of the week, I asked how his rash was. The treatment hadn't worked. He'd have to go back to the dermatologist to get something stronger, but this time he made the appointment.

Tom came back with stronger antibiotics but didn't involve me in the application of the cream this time around. At the end of that week, I asked how his rash was. He said it still wasn't OK; he'd have to get a refill of the second prescription. *Three weeks' worth of oral and topical antibiotics? Was it even a bacterial infection?* I didn't bother inquiring about the rash again, but the seeds of suspicion had been planted.

At the bottom of the same trash can that housed the Viagra packet, I found an invoice from a second dermatologist to the tune of $2500 for laser removal of warts after the end of the aforementioned three-week period. Am I unreasonable to surmise that Tom's incurable rash was related to the warts that had to be removed? Tom later claimed that this entire performance, in which he'd given me a cameo role, had been over a "prostate infection." Men his age get prostate infections and related issues, so why would he lie if he'd gotten one? Furthermore, while I'm no doctor, I'm pretty sure that the prostate isn't located on the upper back or shoulders.

THOSE ROTTEN KIDS!

A couple months before the "prostate infection," Tom bought $1500 of Sony video equipment online. He did this on a credit card for which I wasn't a supplementary cardholder. Because the video equipment wasn't delivered to our home, I didn't find out about this purchase until financial discovery. As was my right, I queried this item. In black and white, Tom denied having anything to do with it and claimed it must have been one of the kids.

There were two glaring problems with this response. First of all, our kids wouldn't have dared spend that sort of money without permission. Second, and more important, their supplementary card spending was itemized under their individual names, and the video equipment purchase was under Tom's own name. No plausible deniability here.

Interestingly, several months earlier, when I was packing up Tom's stuff in my excitement to throw him out of the house, I came across a mini Sony remote control in the pocket of an empty suitcase. I couldn't figure out for the life of me what it was for because all of Tom's devices were Apple. Not knowing its significance at the time, I chucked the remote in the box with all the other unidentifiable electronic doodads. Oops, I have no idea where it is now! Tom is an enterprising fellow, though. I'm sure he's found a replacement remote so that filming of his privately produced documentaries goes smoothly.

After I dropped the matter, Tom complained that I'd questioned the perfectly innocent video equipment purchase he made toward the end of our marriage.

Hold on, Tom. Didn't you say it must have been one of the kids? And why did you arrange for the perfectly innocent video equipment to be delivered somewhere other than home?

Moral of the story: if you're going to tell lies, try to keep them straight.

A BIT OF R & R

There was another fabrication I didn't find out about until financial discovery. This duplicitous act took place three years earlier, at the start of Tom's descent into rampant adultery. Tom had been feeling stressed. The past year hadn't been easy workwise, mainly because he wasn't able to replicate the fabulous success of the previous two years. I recommended he go for a long weekend to a popular spa resort I'd recently visited.

Tom booked it through our travel agent and went, or so I thought. Surreptitiously, he had made alternative transportation arrangements to another city known for its beauty, cultural attractions, and heaving red light district. When I saw from the credit card and bank statements that he'd been in this city for an entire weekend, I was puzzled. He never mentioned having visited the city, the hotel wasn't his usual standard, and there were several large cash withdrawals over that weekend. Of course, I could easily figure out what Tom had gotten up to, but not how he'd gotten away with the detour. How could he have gone to this city without my knowing? My excellent memory finally yielded the answer.

Holy cow. That was the weekend Tom was supposed to have been at the spa! He paid for the expensive spa package but didn't actually use it. That was why he claimed he ordered room service for every meal and had zero recollection of the resort's fabulous health food or the table reserved for single spa-goers. That was why he couldn't describe the instructors at the 9:00 a.m. stretch class, the one he swore he went to every morning without fail. That's why his experience of the acupuncturist didn't remotely resemble mine, not one iota. He didn't do any of these things, so he had to make it all up. Hey, at least he got some recreation.

A SENSE OF RELIEF

I know that Tom went on to manufacture more narratives over the ensuing three years. I see that many earlier stories were fabrications too. What I don't know is how many more I may have missed. So many lies, so much duplicity. How big a sham was my marriage? I'm pretty certain it was a big, fat Anglo-American farce of a marriage.

Shocked friends to whom I ultimately disclosed the horrific reality of my life with Tom were all sure that my misery was greatly compounded by discovering the web of deception spun over years and years. That would stand to reason.

Funnily enough, though, I enjoyed a strange sense of relief when financial discovery and other truth bombs cleared up so much of the confusion I'd felt for thirty years. Trust me when I tell you that *bewilderment* over the relentlessly cruel behavior of someone you love and are devoted to, someone you've built your life with, becomes a debilitating—truly life-draining—condition. I constantly second-guessed my words and actions, I could never relax, and my self-worth scraped along at rock bottom for years. Even the wonderful vacation of my sleeping hours was interrupted by twisted nightmares of strange transgressions and the punishments I so richly deserved. Some nights I didn't even get to sleep.

Dear Reader, does it make any sense to you that discovering the scale of Tom's dishonesty enabled me to view the abuse in a whole new light? Tom was the problem. He was a complete phony, full of baloney. He always had been. The deceit, adultery, and abuse were inextricably linked: the massive effort of being Tom meant that he was compelled to create his own reality in which I was the bad guy, responsible for all foul-ups, imagined or real or possible at some later date. In other words, Tom had to make shit up as he went along so that he had a clear-cut black-and-white narrative he could live with and a malefactor he could blame, punish, and cheat on without a second thought. In his BPD mind, so prone to "splitting," the evil Nunzia got everything that was coming to her.[24]

---

24 This frequent characterization of me as the bad guy was a manifestation of "splitting." According to Priory, a well-established mental health facility in the South of England, "Splitting is a psychological mechanism which allows the [BPD] person to tolerate difficult and overwhelming emotions by seeing someone as good or bad, idealised or devalued. This makes it easier to manage the emotions that they are feeling, which on the surface seem to be contradictory... A [BPD] person may hold onto these black and white views permanently. For others, their opposing views can fluctuate over time, where they switch from seeing someone or something as entirely good to entirely bad, or vice versa." "Splitting in EUPD: Causes, Effects and Support," Priory, May 29, 2023, https://www.priorygroup.com/blog/understanding-splitting-in-borderline-personality-disorder#.

CHAPTER 11

DESTROYING ME AS A WOMAN AND UNDERMINING MY POSITION AS MOTHER

CLUELESS

After we got married and moved abroad, and especially after the birth of our first child, Tom moved inexorably beyond constant impatience and hostility toward a disgust of the woman he initially claimed to adore. I suspect his contempt for me permeated most conversations, but for many years, I didn't recognize the extent or permanence of the rejection. At first, I perceived extreme irritation caused principally by me, a situation I was sure could be remedied when I lost the baby weight and figured out how to be less bothersome. Tom's explosions, while no more extreme than in London, were far more frequent, which, in the thick of it, I didn't register either.

I gave birth to Dominic shortly after arriving at our first posting. I was living a cushy life in a fabulous apartment in a beautiful neighborhood. Tom, in a fit of positivity, expressly asked me to stop working. He said, "We're a team. It's a division of labor. I earn the money. You are in charge of the baby and the home. When you get settled, make some new friends, enjoy some yoga classes." Tom probably meant these words at the time, but soon thereafter it was as though he'd never uttered them. His renewed goodwill evaporated almost instantly.

In hindsight, I speculate that the decline in my status (as I recall, pretty much from the moment I produced *his* son) was the result of some BPD splitting, whereby in Tom's black-and-white mind, I'd become worse than useless. (For more on splitting, please see footnote in Chapter 10.) If it was indeed splitting that Tom was experiencing, I don't know what triggered my transfer to the bad person column. Unless, of course, the dalliance (a form of discarding) while I was in the US with one-year-old Dominic was underway earlier than I realized.

It was difficult for me to adjust to not working—for all of a month. I discovered I wasn't eligible for a work permit anyway, so I graciously accepted this career break. I had an au pair and a housekeeper, which meant plenty of quality time with the baby and no drudgery. With ample opportunity to exercise, I quickly lost that baby weight and got back into shape. I was always well dressed, coiffed, and made-up. I frequently got attention from other men, which I didn't court and always rebuffed. Not once did I receive a compliment from Tom.

I learned the local language and was friendly with the natives and expats. I had an upbeat attitude toward my new home and engaged in none of the negative comparisons so often heard from trailing spouses. I felt fortunate because I was fortunate. Tom had achieved major career success. We enjoyed salary and benefits out the wazoo. And we had a gorgeous little boy.

The stars were completely aligned for us. I should have been having the time of my life, but every morning I woke up off-kilter, apprehension about what the day would bring always niggling away at the back of my mind. Wasn't I doing what I was supposed to be doing?

Tom was often traveling. When he wasn't, he was late getting back from the office. When he got home, he usually snapped or raged at me. He didn't always have something specific to charge me with; he was just letting off steam. *What a relief! It wasn't directed at me.* Sometimes, though, the metaphorical loafer accidentally fell off my foot, and I had to pay for "starting trouble." Either way, the penalty was a bollocking and sometimes a push or slap. Committed by me or not, missteps that wouldn't merit a reaction from most other people whipped Tom into a complete froth even when we'd been having a pleasant time.

I loved my husband. I was attentive to him, which seemed to set him off. I displeased him so frequently. Had he stopped loving me? What had I done? I looked for and found fault in myself. *If only I hadn't mentioned that. If only I'd called him earlier. If only I hadn't called him at all. If only I understood current affairs better. If only I hadn't asked him what time we were supposed to leave the house. If only I'd come across as more enthusiastic. If only I'd come across as less enthusiastic. If only I weren't so clueless and gauche. If only I were prettier. If only I were smarter. If only, if only, if only.*

I was anxious and ashamed but 100 percent focused on overcoming my various deficits so that I could become a more pleasing wife. Even when I understood that Tom's lashing out was independent of anything I'd done, I still felt small and believed it was my responsibility to make things right. I persisted with the delusion that I could implement self-improvements to make Tom happy with me and immunize him against upsets, including those caused by outside circumstances. Using the same tenacity I attacked all challenges with, I'd vanquish Tom's ever-present displeasure. Despite the toll Tom's behavior was taking on me, I normalized the tragic state of our relationship. This sleight of mind allowed me to remain optimistic and appreciative of my circumstances and of Tom. I was his number one supporter.

I was privately thrilled when I managed to distract Tom for a few minutes, getting him to smile or laugh. Honestly, I was wild about Tom and proud of him. He'd made a splash in his industry and, from my skewed perspective, he'd matured dramatically since his irresponsible, petulant business school days. When I got the chance to speak with him about the topics he covered for work, I was riveted because he was so well informed and absolutely brilliant. When Tom wasn't in anti-Nunzia mode, he told me I was his best audience.

I fooled myself into thinking I could stop Tom's almost constant impatience, anger, and explosions by reaching personal perfection and showing undying love in ways that would meet his expectations. I would succeed; I would wipe out the contempt and gain my rightful position as valued wife and mother.

THE BLAME GAME

When I called Tom at work, he was sharp with me. I stopped calling for fear of making him angry, which would then lead to the complaint that I didn't care about him. I formulated a policy of calling after 7:00 p.m. if he hadn't called me first. If he wasn't going out for dinner, the main topic of that phone conversation was always supper at home, namely that he didn't want any. He'd had a big lunch, *and was I trying to make him fat or give him a heart attack?* I reassured him he didn't have to eat. He could just sit with me while I ate. I had this weird thing about husbands and wives having supper together, that's all.

It was uncanny how often this conversation was repeated throughout those early years and then picked up again and unremittingly pursued for the final decade of our marriage. It was a sick dance. Tom's constant early evening refrain was *I'm not eating anything.* My housekeeper and I quickly learned that we had to have something put aside because his resolve would falter, and he'd ask if there was a little "soupçon" for him. Tom's soupçon of a healthy meal was often followed by an entire tub of ice cream. Dear Reader, I hope you realize this paragraph isn't about Tom's unhealthy eating habits.

This first posting abroad was a big job, one that got even bigger when, yet again, Tom managed to get his boss fired. Therefore, within six months of arriving, he was covering two positions, a workload he had the intellect and stamina to cope with. In fact, he put in a stellar performance and was recognized for his success, including through obscene bonuses.

Pulling off this stellar performance was no mean feat, however. Being transferred abroad at the age of just twenty-nine, Tom went from supervising two junior associates in London to managing an international staff of several dozen almost overnight. When Tom thrust himself into these roles, where would he have suddenly gained the wisdom or fortitude to navigate the rapid, massive change in his career trajectory or the challenges of managing a large team? I had full faith in Tom at the time, but I can now recognize that the effort of getting the job done and keeping his shit together overwhelmed him emotionally. Of course, no one at work was aware of Tom's inability to cope because he made sure to keep all rage and frustration tightly under wraps until he got home to me. I'm also quite sure Tom never acknowledged to himself that he wasn't coping well, despite the anger he carted home from work on an almost daily basis.

One stressor Tom did acknowledge, though, was Richard, an older colleague who helped Tom stage the coup against his boss. By all accounts, Richard was an accomplished Machiavellian prick who was even more skilled than Tom in the dark arts of office politics and better connected within the organization. Tom had more than met his match in Richard, who was an ally for only as long as it took to remove Tom's boss. Until Tom switched firms and countries, he was in an almost constant state of outrage about Richard's duplicity. As far as Tom was concerned, every encounter with Richard was fraught with malice and treachery.

Tom often arrived home too het up to elaborate on Richard's atrocity du jour, but he wasn't so tied up in knots that he couldn't exact revenge—on me. I took Richard's consequences for him, getting screamed at while cornered in the kitchen or bathroom. One Saturday afternoon, completely out of the blue, Tom accused me of thinking that Richard was a good guy, when all I'd done—a whole week earlier—was report that Richard had greeted me pleasantly and attempted small talk at a recent social event. Tom didn't accept my clarification because, in his overwrought mind, I was already in league with the enemy, someone I'd met exactly two times. Due to this alleged alliance, I earned a frenzied verbal attack followed by a firm slap across the face.

In a quiet moment the next day, I stood up to Tom. At this point, I was still capable of expressing righteous indignation in extreme circumstances. I told Tom his work-related meltdowns targeted at me had to end. I was a supportive wife, always there to listen. He could unload his frustrations but not abuse me verbally or physically. Tom said he was sorry. *Sorry, but...* "Nunzia, you have no idea what it's like to work with this arsehole. He's trying to destroy me... He's going to succeed in getting rid of our country head... He's a nasty piece of work... If you had to work with him, you'd be fucking angry too."

I was tempted to say, "Welcome to the real world, Tom, where there are assholes galore." His *Sorry, but* had worked him into a lather all over again, so I merely repeated that he needed to stop. He stood down, but the hostility never dissipated.

Sincere but fleeting apologies topped off by blame-shifting are typical ploys of many BPD sufferers. Accepting responsibility is too much for their delicate self-images to bear, so the people they "love" must relieve them of this burden. My general culpability had taken root back in business school when I'd done the work and Tom hadn't, and it continued to sprout and spread. In a grown-up environment of constant stress, my mere existence was now the noxious weed that was marring his entire yard. Yanking me up when I "started trouble" or when something, anything, went wrong was not enough for Tom; he needed to make repeated applications of weed killer to destroy me.

OUT OF FAVOR

At the five-year mark, several months before we moved on to our second posting, I reached the clear-eyed conclusion that Tom regretted settling for me. I was sure that Tom's fury at having plain, mediocre, unexciting Nunzia as his wife was his number one stressor. Now that he was successful in the big, wide world, he could do far better. That was the message I took when he made pointed comparisons to other women. *So-and-so's wife is absolutely stunning! Why can't you dress like her? Why can't you be as organized as so-and-so? You should learn from so-and-so's wife how to hold dinner parties.* On top of Tom's neglect and rage, I quietly absorbed this criticism. My conclusion: I was seen wanting and had fallen out of favor.

I wrote Tom a letter, offering him an amicable divorce whereby I'd stay close with the kids. I didn't want him to be so unhappy or have my kids grow up in such stress. He read it, crumpled it up in a ball, threw it away, and then said I was wrong, stupid in fact. *Why was I starting trouble? He hadn't settled for me.* But he never went to the effort of hearing me out or proving me wrong. He never thought about why I'd reached this conclusion. I wasn't a priority.

You see, except for the relatively calm hiatus of Tom's "Christian years" and the abject misery of our final years when he hated the sight of me, I was actively scorned but essential to the enterprise. I was the vessel for *his* three children, the household administrative assistant, and the cat he could conveniently kick when he walked through the door. Only in hindsight can I recognize just how damaging this period was for me and how it laid the groundwork for the shell of a woman I was to become.

Having had my offer of an amicable divorce summarily dismissed, I submissively packed up home and family and went to the considerable effort of getting us reestablished in our new posting. This might be a fresh start. *Yeah, right.* The evil Richard was replaced by other bastards, so there was always something for Tom to rage about. Fortunately, Tom had to travel even more for his new regional role, staying away for a week, sometimes two to three weeks, at a time. Several times a year, therefore, I could enjoy stretches of peace and quiet and pretend that all was well. In the run-up to Tom's return, I shrank into myself, my stomach became upset, and my arms stiffened and ached.

On the face of it, our circumstances had changed drastically. The new posting couldn't have been more different from the first, so there was plenty to discover and be excited about: a new language to learn, another culture to adjust to, people to meet. Tom was earning a lot more money and perks and was even more powerful. But he was still angry, and I clearly still had an uncanny knack for starting trouble. *Plus ça change...*

In silence and bewilderment, I continued to be buffeted about by Tom's unpredictable and capricious nastiness. As I look back on the first year of our second posting, I recognize that I'd almost certainly sunk into "major depressive disorder," though I knew nothing about depression of any type. I developed severe stomach problems. I had a hard time getting out of bed in the morning and took two-hour naps during the day. I couldn't muster enough concentration to read a book. I kept to myself and didn't cultivate any friendships. I took pleasure in almost nothing. When Tom was out of town, I aimlessly roamed the streets of my new city in the early evening, returning home only when all the shops had closed. The losers during my low ebb were Dominic, Louisa, and baby Jamie, who were fortunately lovingly cared for in my absence by a housekeeper and a nanny.

Besides not recognizing depression in myself, I wasn't a recluse by nature. I was ready for something to shift when—fortuitously—the head of the PTA at Dominic's school asked me to run a committee. In fact, she did me a tremendous service by assigning me this minor role, which I attacked with energy and enthusiasm. I got validation from other adults, found friends, and established a social life I could enjoy on my own or include Tom in if he was in the mood. Reengagement with life was a virtuous circle. I volunteered for other duties at school, took language courses, and joined a book club. Most important, I also stepped up as a mother. I could never make up for the lost year, but I could rededicate myself to giving my children the happiest upbringing circumstances would allow.

I forged a joyful life for myself, and for several years, it was joyful. I didn't pretend away my rocky relationship with Tom, but I did a good job of compartmentalizing it and hiding it from others. Of course, I quietly persevered with my goal of becoming the perfect wife to Tom so that we could all live happily ever after.

TRUSSED UP LIKE A CHRISTMAS TURKEY

This is the first time I'm sharing this shameful story with anyone. I haven't even shared it with my psychiatrist. I simply cannot bring myself to utter with my own voice what happened to me. Somehow typing the words out is more clinical, easier to execute.

Tom was in a quiet sort of funk, which was highly unusual for him. I felt he needed some inspiration, so I bought myself a piece of sexy lingerie. It was lacy, tasteful, and a tad suggestive, nothing the Kardashians wouldn't wear on Instagram. I put it on and waited for Tom in bed. He climbed in and threw open the covers. He started to guffaw—and guffawed and guffawed. When he was finally able to get words out of his mouth, he told me I looked trussed up, just like a Christmas turkey. When he finished wiping the tears of hilarity out of his eyes, he told me to take it off.

Tom occasionally reminded me of the time I'd been trussed up like a Christmas turkey. He would guffaw with the memory. *Wasn't it hilarious?* I just stitched on a smile, forcing myself not to weep from abject shame and self-consciousness. I never recovered from this humiliation.

WHAT A JOKER!

After the anecdote above, perhaps you think me too sensitive, the kind of gal who can't take a joke. In fact, except for this knee-slapper, I wasn't the butt of Tom's pernicious jokes until the final years of our marriage.

However, Tom often made jokes about his sister Camilla to her face, especially about her intellectual abilities. He'd then finish his repartee with "only joking!" Camilla wasn't remotely stupid, though, proving to be a wise and articulate observer on many topics. She railed against these "jokes," explaining that both the content and frequency of Tom's witticisms were a sign of gross disrespect toward her. I rolled my eyes at her sensitivity and, along with Tom, viewed her reactions as absurd.

I finally twigged what Tom had been doing to Camilla all along when I became the brunt of Tom's jokes. My intellectual abilities, my weight and appearance, and my lack of talent all provided perfect material for Tom's humor.

Making jokes that hit too close to the bone and then chuckling and/or proclaiming that the butt of the joke needs to "relax" is an insidious form of devaluing that needs to be recognized as emotional abuse.

UGLY BITCH

One morning early in our final posting, I said or did something to displease Tom before he left for work. Remember: I was on constant high alert to avoid making him angry or even provoking the smallest impatience. I even skipped simple questions requiring simple answers because I never knew what would make Tom fly off the handle on any given day.

It's not that I don't remember what happened on this particular morning; at the time I didn't know what I'd done. Whatever it was, it must have been bad—so bad that Tom was forced to call me an ugly bitch as he stomped out the door to work. I was horrified to learn that I was ugly or to think that my husband found me ugly or that he would want to hurt me so badly that he would say such a thing, even if he didn't mean it.

I had errands to run, so I picked myself up, literally and figuratively, got dressed, and headed to the city center. The show must go on. I got out of the taxi and headed to the bank. I never made it because the enormity of the insult descended upon me. As I crossed the street, I imagined that everyone was staring at me in my hideousness. I needed to disappear quickly. With tears and mascara streaming down my face, I ran back to the taxi rank and headed home.

At this point, Tom still had a conscience. Upon reaching the office, he recognized the damage he'd done and sent a bouquet of flowers with a note of sincere apology. I was still shocked to the core but open to his contrition.

My response was to come up with a private to-do list (updated edition) to make myself more attractive and agreeable so that Tom would never need to say this again. I read all manner of self-help books. I went to an image consultant who helped me become more stylish. I became a slave to the gym and yoga. I chronicled my daily successes and failures, making ever more ambitious goals for myself. It was a life of second-guessing and constant striving. When I go through my journals from that period, I almost weep for the woman who lived for a man she'd never succeed in pleasing.

YOU'RE TOO UGLY TO BE SO FUCKING RUDE

I had to wait about eighteen months until the next devastating insult. We were visiting friends in another city for an important family celebration that included a set of visiting grandparents. We had to leave the hotel by 10:00 a.m. to make the church service. Uncharacteristically, I was completely ready ahead of our planned departure. Tom, though, had once again cut it finely by going to the gym and then showering at the time we should have been walking out the door.

I asked Tom if it would be OK for me to call the front desk to order a taxi. If we left in the next couple of minutes, we'd have a chance of making it for the first half of the church service, but I didn't say this to Tom. Maybe he was a mind reader because his response, yelled with the hotel room door open, was that I was too fucking ugly to be so rude.

Because it was clear that things were only going to deteriorate from there, I left the room and went down to the front desk, where an employee quickly got me a taxi. Tom appeared ten minutes later, still furious. I said nothing at all during the taxi ride, feeling crushed and humiliated. Tom was unaffected and continued to tear me down.

At the lunch afterward, Tom was the very picture of charm, especially with the visiting grandparents, whom he felt a particular need to impress. I, on the other hand, was on autopilot just trying to get through the day without bursting into tears. I could barely function. I was unable to laugh or engage with anyone. I honestly wondered, *How will I survive this?* This time there wasn't even an apology from Tom. It was settling in on me that I was a repulsive and unworthy piece of shit. This was about the time I started dressing in black, standing on the periphery at social events, and covering my lower face with my hand whenever possible. I didn't want to be noticed.

CROSSING THE RUBICON

I believe that calling me ugly that second time was the crossing of the Rubicon for Tom. After that incident, Tom felt little need to hold back devastating personal insults—beyond the usual labels of *fucking bitch*, *fucking old lady*, *pharisaical hypocrite*, and *liar*, which had long ceased to mean anything to me. Tom was now committed to a course of action: to destroy me and grind me down with diatribes that could escalate in seconds, last for hours, and pop up again in the ensuing weeks or days when I thought there could be nothing left unsaid on that topic. I've already told you that I was held personally responsible for just about every incident that made Tom angry, but we'd entered a whole new dimension. His rage was so personal and relentless that I must have been the cause. It wasn't just the frequency of my troublemaking; Tom's rage was entrenched, the cumulative result of dealing with a wife who was and always had been a low-quality person.

When the kids were all in big school, I went back to work part-time. If I had a problem at the office, Tom never heard me out. Not once. He didn't need to because he knew the problem lay with me. He would instantly kick off, attributing 100 percent of the fault to me and my flaws, my deficits being both intellectual and moral. As Tom became more successful, he felt even more certainty and entitlement, allowing him to exercise zero restraint in passing judgment and delivering his verdicts in any way he deemed appropriate, including publicly.

When I started my own business toward the end of Tom's "Christian years," I occasionally asked him for advice because I valued his wisdom. Sometimes he was tremendously helpful and generous with his time, but the advice often grew into unsolicited opinions on unrelated matters. I had to take the rough with the smooth, though, and at least he was attempting to be patient with his less able wife. Tom frequently reminded me that I needed to take his advice. He knew what he was doing.

As Tom grew out of his Christianity, he achieved new heights of disapproval. A question from me was no longer just the opportunity for impatient sighs and harsh statements about my poor judgment in professional situations. It was the launching pad for Tom to savage *everything* I did in any realm, with his running commentary based on ignorance, assumptions, and outdated information, but mainly his total contempt for me.

As you can imagine, dear Reader, I stopped asking for advice or even talking about my business. But that didn't prove an impediment to Tom. One morning, three and a half years before our marriage ended, Tom thought it would be a good idea to raise the subject of my poor business decision-making, unprompted and as he was running out the door to a client meeting. He became so unhinged about my stupidity that he couldn't stop himself. It was only when he realized he'd gone on for so long that he was already fifteen minutes late for his meeting that he ended his savaging of me. As soon as he stormed out, I packed and moved to a hotel. The next day, I flew to meet my girlfriends in Italy for cooking lessons as previously planned. I didn't know what else to do. When my week in Italy was finished, I flew back home to the same old, same old.

During this later phase, Tom's complete and utter losses of control (as opposed to brief or protracted explosions) became weekly occurrences. Indeed, looking back at the arc of Tom's behavior, I can say that his late-stage meltdowns were of a different nature from those that occurred during our first two decades together. In the early years, Tom's instability and unreasonableness were the behavior of an immature, desperate, angry young man trying to find his place in the world. Once his corporate career was on its upward trajectory, Tom's anger and nastiness were the behavior of a more mature and aware jerk deeply resentful that he was answerable to fucking morons who had no idea what they were doing.

The Tom I was dealing with now was older, richer, even more sure of himself, and—dare I say it—evil. It was no longer merely the case that Tom's irritation frequently boiled over into shit fits of varying degrees that traumatized me. It was way, way beyond that. He became a horrible person who felt zero need to control himself—ever. The demon of BPD seemed to have taken Tom over, and he was reveling in it. While I cannot state this with any certainty, he appeared to have defied the typical trajectory of BPD, whereby the affliction, according to the Mayo Clinic, can ameliorate over time.[25] In middle age, Tom hadn't mellowed. On the contrary, he'd

---

25 "Borderline personality disorder usually begins by early adulthood. The condition is most serious in young adulthood. Mood swings, anger, and impulsiveness often get better with age. But the main issues of self-image and fear of being abandoned, as well as relationship issues, go on." "Borderline Personality Disorder," Mayo Clinic, January 31, 2024, https://www.mayoclinic.org/diseases-conditions/borderline-personality-disorder/symptoms-causes/syc-20370237.

become absolutely bonkers, stark raving mad, and utterly infatuated with his wicked, deviant, self-absorbed, chaotic lifestyle.

I'd known for three decades that speaking up for myself wasn't only a waste of my time but also gave Tom some extra insubordination to quash. Nonetheless, my ill-considered inclination in the final stretch of our relationship was to continue to attempt to gently correct his misapprehensions during the brief pauses in his tirades. Tom obviously wasn't having it. He'd erupt that I shouldn't "justify" myself. I'd then fall into line with "Tom, you're right." And I'd stand there and listen for however long it took for him to finish criticizing, issuing orders, and destroying me—patiently waiting for him to remove his pickax from what little confidence and self-esteem I had left—so that I could remove myself from his presence. The duration of my punishment depended on how much time Tom had at his disposal. The magnitude of my punishment had no constraints, though. As you'll read below, Tom's venom and hatred toward me were beyond anything that most of us have ever personally experienced.

INCOMPETENT FUCKING LOSER

It hardly seems possible, but Tom's anger and contempt toward me continued to escalate. When triggered, he needed to throw everything, including my nationality, into the admixture for the purpose of assassinating my character. He could vomit out his ugliness without drawing breath. When most of us would have burned ourselves out or fumbled for just the right insults, Tom could go on and on, demonstrating both stamina and originality in his performances.

There was one phrase he coined about three to four years before our split and then relied upon because it felt so good to enunciate and applied to me so well: *incompetent fucking loser*. He hurled this epithet at me hundreds of times, including in front of the children.

Ultimately, Tom's hatred of me was a force that took him over and made me hypervigilant, to the extent that I planned my movements around the house. I stayed out of his way, except when he commanded me to be in his presence. It's not clear why he wanted me in a room with him because my very existence enraged him.

The stress of the waking hours carried into the hours we should have been sleeping. The anxiety of living with Tom was causing me insomnia and making me physically ill. Tom wanted me in bed at the same time as him because he was a light sleeper. If I came into the room after he was in bed, I'd wake him up. Tom's demand was completely understandable, but I was becoming unable to sleep. Lying right next to Tom, knowing that I was an incompetent fucking loser, was no doubt a factor. Many a night, I'd stare at the ceiling for a couple hours before crawling out of bed to go to another room to work on the computer or watch TV. If I woke Tom up, which I sometimes did, I could expect a long-drawn-out and full-scale bollocking.

There were other occasions when I managed to get to sleep only to be woken by Tom, who needed to scream at me because he was angry about something that had happened earlier. One time, he woke me up because he needed my advice and comfort. God help me if I'd ever woken him for any reason whatsoever.

YOU'RE NOT WORTHY OF RESPECT, NUNZIA

I attributed my low position in the household to things that happened when the kids were adolescents and teenagers, but, truth be told, the rot started far earlier. As mentioned in Chapter 3, when a small child sees one parent abusing the other, he may come to see the victim as the culprit. When this dynamic is a child's constant diet, he'll understand that it's the correct way to behave toward the victim. In our family's case, that culpable victim was me.

Everyone in the household, including our housekeeper, picked up on the vibe and wouldn't hesitate to scream and swear at me.

I'm deeply scarred by having children whom I loved and nurtured, dropped everything for, and thought I'd raised well, treat me like dirt. When I told Tom, toward the end of our marriage, of my despair that none of the children treated me with respect, I naively expected sympathy and support. What I got instead was "Nunzia, the children don't treat you with respect because you're not worthy of respect." End of subject. I was crushed. There was no possible retort.

LET'S LEAVE THIS FUCKING BITCH ON HER OWN

The undermining played out with each child in a different way, depending on their personalities, ages, and what Tom was trying to accomplish at that point. When Jamie was fourteen, I asked him to clean up the mess he'd made in the TV room. He immediately began shouting, informing me that it wasn't a convenient time for him to tidy up and that I was too fussy anyway. Of course, I was angry to be overridden by my own child in my own home. However, there was no mileage in arguing with such an aggressive personality, so I told him I'd deal with the mess myself.

Jamie wasn't having it and continued to yell at me. I didn't respond in kind but instead urged him to hang out in his room. We could discuss things when "we" calmed down. He'd learned well from Tom. He was going to prevail with his own mother, who wasn't prepared to argue with a fourteen-year-old. Jamie continued to pummel me. He felt I was answerable to him.

Ten minutes into this nightmare, Tom walked in. I thought he'd step in to handle it. He handled it all right. He asked no questions. Instead, he immediately took Jamie's side and called me a fucking bitch. Jamie chimed in and agreed that I was a fucking bitch.

Then Tom said, "Let's leave this fucking bitch on her own."

Just like that, they left me on my own with my mouth hanging open in shock. They proceeded to the master bedroom, making sure I heard their ongoing chorus of "What a fucking bitch."

THE TEENAGE YEARS THAT WENT ON AND ON

Louisa was a particular heartbreak to me. Her horrible teenage years lasted from the age of eleven until she was at least twenty-three. Tom assured me that this was normal, but I knew it wasn't. Our daughter was a sweet, sweet child, and then one day she found a voice—an ugly, malevolent voice encouraged by her father.

Louisa was spoiled and knew that Tom would get her whatever she asked for. Even if she didn't ask, he'd provide the top of the line of anything. Once, after a trip to New York City with Daddy, she opened her suitcase to reveal a $500 DKNY silk top, two pairs of Tory Burch flats, and a bunch of crap from Abercrombie & Fitch. She was thirteen and still growing. I was incensed by Tom's largesse. This girl didn't even bother hanging up her clothes; they stayed on the floor until she needed them ironed or the housekeeper and I couldn't stand it any longer.

When Louisa did "tidy up," she simply transferred the clothes from the floor to the dirty clothes hamper. Once, when she was sixteen and even Tom was complaining about her messes, I went into her room to help her organize. I brought hangers and chirped that we'd start by putting the stuff that was still clean in some sort of order in the closet. She immediately threw a tantrum, shrieking that she didn't know how to put things on a hanger.

I calmly told her I'd show her how and that we'd finish in no time! Louisa continued to shriek. Tom then entered the room and immediately announced, "Nunzia, you've caused yet another train wreck." Tom invoked my ability to cause a train wreck again and again, and this girl knew she was onto a good thing.

I won't regale you with the dozens of other stunts Louisa got away with. A single boarding school anecdote will suffice to demonstrate the sick dynamic in our family. The girl was so blithe and careless that she took her computer into the shower cubicle and placed it on the changing bench. Why did she have her computer in the shower cubicle? Because she couldn't get ready without music. Anybody with a brain would know that the steam from the shower would work its way into the laptop, eventually ruining it.

When the laptop finally broke down, Louisa discovered her brain and called her father, not me. Tom said, "Of course, Darling, I'll buy you a new computer when you come back for spring break." I didn't know this promise from Daddy was a done deal. Therefore, when I rang to tell Louisa about her transportation arrangements, I instructed her to bring her old computer home. We'd be taking it to the clever IT guys in our town who could fix just about anything. A volcanic eruption ensued. "But Daddy is buying me a new computer as soon as I get back!" she screamed. I responded that she could have a new computer if the old one couldn't be fixed. Louisa hung up in a complete strop, of course.

When I brought this issue up with Tom, he crumpled his face and said, "But I promised her."

I was feeling bold that day and retorted that he should have promised her nothing. We were doing her no favors by letting her get away with such irresponsibility.

"If the computer can't be fixed," I suggested, "how about letting her use the communal one in the school library? That would teach her to be a better steward of her things!"

More of Tom's puppy dog face. He agreed in principle, but I knew I was already defeated. Louisa brought her old computer home. It couldn't be fixed because the hard drive had indeed been destroyed by the daily intake of steam. Daddy took her out to buy a new and completely upgraded Apple laptop, which had always been Louisa's endgame.

THE BOSTON DUCK

I suffered from a medical condition that wasn't immediately life-threatening but needed to be dealt with. The doctors in my locale recommended I go to Massachusetts General Hospital in Boston to get treatment available only in the US. Getting from our summer place on Cape Cod to Boston was relatively easy, so I booked an hour with a specialist at Mass General for early August, just before she left for her own vacation.

Tom agreed to drive me to the hospital, but I didn't bother asking him to attend the consultation with me—and he didn't offer. Over the previous four years, he'd accompanied me to three appointments, waited in the lobby during a four-hour surgery, and flown out the next day. Tom mentally kept score, and I was fully aware he'd reached the limit of the time and energy he'd devote to this Nunzia project.

Always killing as many birds as possible and never wasting his precious time—except when watching sports, walking the golf course, enjoying the nineteenth hole, or viewing internet porn—Tom decided that our trip to Boston had to include some tourist experiences for the English relatives.

Only on the appointment day did I find out that Mass General had become an inconvenient detour for Tom and our visitors. They were kindly accommodating my needs by parking at a garage in the general vicinity of the hospital. The trip had morphed into a sightseeing junket through the streets of Boston and down the Charles River on the amphibious army vehicle known as the Boston Duck. Tom had purchased the Boston Duck tickets online, and his updated itinerary meant I had to be dropped off more than an hour and a half before my scheduled appointment and reappear at the parking garage for our drive back to the Cape forty-five minutes after the start of my scheduled appointment.

"Do not be late," I was admonished. From the parking garage, I headed to the hospital to register, hoping this world-renowned specialist could see me early. She couldn't. I got in to see her ten minutes later than scheduled, which gave me less than half an hour for a proper consultation on my first visit with her.

I explained my time constraint and kept an eye on my watch. She went quickly through the plan of invasive treatments she had in store for me. I figured I could ask crucial follow-up questions by email. She looked on with alarm and pity as I abruptly stood up and said I'd be in touch. I bolted past reception, called over to say I'd phone with a credit card number to settle the bill, and ran to the parking garage.

As I approached, Tom was making a right turn off the exit ramp. They were leaving Boston without me. I flailed my arms and yelled.

My sister-in-law spotted me and told Tom I was coming. He didn't come to a full stop, but he did slow down so that I could get into the ridiculous rented Range Rover. I had to open the door myself.

As I attempted to clamber up and in, Louisa didn't appreciate that I was forced to shove my big bag of medical records onto her lap. She demanded to know what I thought I was doing. She then swiped the bag off her lap onto the floor, which meant my ascent into the car was further delayed as I avoided stepping on the films.

When I finally made it into my seat, I was in genuine distress, an emotion I'd become proficient at concealing. This time, though, I couldn't stop the tears and asked Tom why he hadn't instructed Louisa to help me get into the moving car rather than allowing her to hinder me.

My sobbing was met with a shrieking and entirely unsympathetic response from Tom. "How dare you blame this on me? I did tell her to move!"

"Well, you piped up only after you saw that I was holding *you* up," I had the gall to retort through my wails. My impulsive willingness to stand up to Tom led to a spectacular loss of control, this one definitely earning a place in his Top Five Meltdowns.

Tom began to rant and rave and swear at me. We were soon in a tunnel with what seemed to me a dozen lanes of converging traffic. While his shoulders heaved and his body convulsed in rage, he sped up and abruptly slowed down. He swerved inside our lane. He swerved between lanes. After three to four minutes of this, he threw on the brakes and told me to get out of his fucking car. Right there in the tunnel, with plenty of early evening traffic flowing behind us.

It was a surreal moment. I opened the door to get out.

Under normal circumstances, I'd have been embarrassed by the inconvenience we were causing others. However, I was in shock and impervious to the gawking faces in the other lanes. It flashed through my mind that I'd find it very difficult to get back to the Cape on my own and that I'd have some serious explaining to do when the Massachusetts State Police showed up to find out why this crazy woman was walking in what was clearly a non-pedestrian zone. But I was a desperate, defeated woman who wanted to be anywhere but in that Range Rover.

When Tom saw that I was climbing out, he applied the accelerator. As he screamed at me to get the fuck back in the car, I was able to slam the door shut so that I didn't fall out. I suspect Tom realized that he, too, would have some serious explaining to do to the Massachusetts State Police about why he'd "dropped me off," especially with so many witnesses to his reckless behavior.

Needless to say, Tom raged the remainder of the way home and right up to the time we had to head over to the neighbors' for an evening cocktail cruise. Neither Louisa nor the English relatives had a word to say to comfort me or chastise Tom. They knew which side their bread was buttered on. The glaring fact that he'd been about to leave Boston without me was never discussed.

ALL PART OF THE MASTER PLAN

In hindsight, I believe that my success with my own little business—tiny compared to Tom's—was a major point against me. Since I was an incompetent fucking loser, I had to be a failure in every realm: holding dinner parties, raising children, being a good wife, organizing the household, and, of course, running a business. If I suggested A, Tom was honor bound to say that A was absolutely wrong and that I needed to do B.

When I hired a young woman because I saw potential in her, Tom vehemently denounced this hiring decision. She was too young, not proven, and a waste of time. However, my decision was soon vindicated: she was highly intelligent, diligent, and proactive. After two and a half very productive years, she resigned to go to graduate school. Tom was then angry with me for losing such a fabulous employee. I explained I'd always expected her to move on. She'd done a great job, and I was very appreciative that she'd helped my company get to the next level. I added that you can't fault people for wanting to fulfill their potential! But Tom was determined to blame me for the loss of this employee, the one whose hiring he was sure was a stupid move in the first place.

Naturally, I made mistakes and bad decisions, which Tom was all too happy to seize on. I always concurred with his flawless judgment, saying, "Yes, Tom, you're absolutely correct. I shouldn't have done that, and I'm sorry," but I was talking to a wall. He'd repeat his refrain of what an incompetent fucking loser I was and throw in that I was "stuffed with pride" to boot because I "didn't take advice."

Regarding my business, as with every other endeavor I undertook, I should have realized far earlier that caving to Tom's accusations of incompetence, accepting culpability, apologizing profusely, acquiescing to his mandatory advice, stoically taking it on the chin, or all of the above was completely futile. No matter how I handled an attack, Tom was going to annihilate me. How did he get away with this time and again, and why did he even want to? If this is what you're asking, you're thinking about Tom and people like him in precisely the wrong way.

As I told you at the very beginning of this book, logic is the worst enemy of the abuser. And logic is an enemy he is hell-bent on defeating. Moreover, your reliance on logic serves to weaken your position; he instinctively knows you believe that all of us usually act in rational and constructive ways. Your misconception about human nature, and his individual nature, renders you powerless against this insane, opportunistic, and malevolent destroyer. He's going to use your beliefs to savage you. Over the months and years, any effective defense falls by the wayside, and your ongoing capitulation serves to embolden him. Remember, the abuser operates in the realm of personal totalitarianism. He knows that success begets success, and he builds on every victory over you. Worse, he redoubles his efforts against you when you've contradicted him or thwarted any of his plans.

HIRING MY REPLACEMENT

Tom felt I was such an incompetent fucking loser that I was incapable of running my own business. Behind my back, he promised the job of CEO of my company to a disaffected male employee reporting directly to his business partner. I furtively dug my heels in and delayed contacting this fellow, whom I suspected Tom was "rescuing" to boost his own ego.

After much haranguing from Tom, I was ultimately forced to call this young man. When I did, I discovered that our proposed meeting wasn't an interview as far as he was concerned but, rather, a hammering out of his package, including how much equity he would get. I was angry but not shocked by Tom's machinations.

I was as noncommittal as possible and made sure I couldn't find any time to meet this fellow. Fortunately, Tom was traveling and otherwise engaged during this period. My replacement eventually recognized that the opportunity to take over my business wasn't going to materialize. Shortly thereafter, he moved to another city to seek fame and fortune.

Still convinced of my inadequacies across the board, Tom—again, behind my back—offered the CEO job to a friend of mine, whom he believed to be an astute businesswoman. My friend felt uncomfortable with this proposition, knowing that Tom hadn't consulted me. In addition, she knew that she was somewhat compromised because Tom—again, behind my back and using joint marital funds—had given her a business loan. She declined Tom's job offer and told me of both the loan and his nefarious plans to replace me. Unfortunately, this clever woman has lost her business and, close to retirement age, is stuck in a formerly great city, languishing in an apartment provided by her ninety-five-year-old father.

Meanwhile, I've been forced to keep on truckin' and have managed somehow without the relentless stream of gratuitous, supercilious, and nonoptional business advice from Tom. My lonely struggle to survive physically, emotionally, and financially has restored some of my self-belief. Moreover, I used the COVID-19 years to my advantage to thrive in my niche. I haven't set the world alight, but I've increased profits and earned accolades from my clients for managing disruptions ethically and efficiently. Not bad for an incompetent fucking loser.

CHAPTER 12

THE FINAL THREE YEARS: HELL ON EARTH

UNMITIGATED CHAOS

It's difficult for me to say with absolute certainty where the "beginning of the end" lay. Nevertheless, in the final three years a conspicuous deterioration in Tom's behavior coincided with his insufferable sense of entitlement and descent into a range of ruinous habits. In any case, I hope I have the distance and perspective to provide an accurate portrayal of the final stage of our marriage. What I'm going for is a picture of pandemonium for me, for the kids, for Tom, and for his clients and colleagues.

Pandemonium wasn't just a symptom of Tom's activities; it was now a desired outcome. Pandemonium was itself a drug for Tom. The fleeting thrill he experienced when he caused chaos was the springboard for further bad behavior and even more ridiculous gestures.

Tom lived his whole life with inner shame, which, in my view, is a sure route to perdition. For as long as I knew him, he sought to impress others in a variety of grandiose—sometimes truly kind, sometimes senselessly munificent, sometimes wildly inappropriate—ways to compensate for the deep, abiding spiritual wounds and feelings of inadequacy that reside in the souls of many suffering from cluster B personality disorders.

In this final stage, Tom's grandiosity became monstrous, causing him to be insanely generous to the wrong people for the wrong reasons and leading him to engage in the sort of profligacy frequently exhibited by lottery winners. Not only did Tom squander a massive chunk or our wealth and inflict tremendous damage on his business; he also made a fool of himself in front of his colleagues, his industry, and probably those who took advantage of his generosity. It was pandemonium played out publicly.

Because of Tom's tone deafness, misplaced sense of superiority, and need to protect himself from the truth, I'm quite certain he's never fully cottoned on to the opprobrium he brought on himself and his family. Furthermore, he's never delved into the reasons he spiraled out of control, first and foremost because he's never admitted to himself that he was out of control. By all accounts, Tom considers his behavior in the final years of our marriage and their aftermath, during which he entered into a serious long-term relationship with an escort who took him for as much as she could, just a minor lapse in judgment.

How did snobby, snotty Tom end up with the sort of gal he'd have sniggered about if one of his mates had glommed on to her and paraded her around town? Part of the answer lies in his likely pathology: a feature identified in many BPD sufferers is the need to fit in with the group they are socializing with at the time. Armed with this information, I can look back and see changes in Tom's behavior for what they were: reflections of the people and forces that were influencing him daily.

SOCIAL INFLUENCERS

Who were the influencers in Tom's life during the final three years of our marriage? Not the Christian men he'd been so close to several years earlier. Certainly not the many excellent, wonderfully diverse friends we made during our marriage, some of whom Tom alienated with his ugly behavior. (In fact, if Tom ran into any of those folks today, he'd be hard-pressed to recall their names or even where he knew them from.) Not his mother's family, whom he'd rightly admired for their kindness, manners, and unfailing decency. Not the social class he identified with for a good chunk of his life. And definitely not me.

A highly influential influencer during those final three years was a very naughty trader who, according to Tom, had a substance abuse problem and wreaked havoc in the lives of his ex-wife and small children. Tom was originally his client. Tom hired him, fired him, and apparently rehired him. I guess the lure of this fellow's antics was too great for Tom to resist.

Another influencer was a former boss who popped up in Tom's professional life again and again like a jack-in-the-box. This fellow, a highly intelligent middle-class chap who did extremely well for himself and now spends his dotage as a Church of England vicar, makes a favorable impression with his impeccable manners and self-deprecating sense of humor. However, I've come to know the depths of this devoted family man's immorality, including his fun suggestions for mixing business with pleasure and his willingness to be economical with the truth in situations where nothing but the truth is demanded.

Yet another influencer during this period was an even older ex-boss Tom appointed to his board. In his late sixties, John was on his third marriage and third litter. One of Tom's employees and I remarked on John's obvious eyelid surgery, Botox injections, dyed hair, and expensive veneers that made his teeth look like two rows of Chiclets. We agreed that John was fooling no one; he looked ridiculous. Tom laughed uncomfortably at our observation.

I wasn't to know that the wheels were already turning in Tom's head. *This old geezer has successfully held back the years and nabbed himself a young and attractive third wife.* In the intervening years, Tom has arranged for some rejuvenation himself.

A couple we knew socially was an especially pernicious pair of influencers. I learned that these two, along with some eminent medical professionals in town, were into the spanky-spankies and swinging. I stupidly forewarned Tom of their activities because he regularly met clients at the bar of the hotel where this salubrious society rented suites for the night. It never occurred to me that he'd use my heads-up to become chummy with this couple, whom he barely remembered when I first mentioned them. Goodness knows how many other influencers Tom encountered in their midst.

I met some of Tom's new friends when he summoned me to the bar to rescue him from "a gang of floozies" (Tom's words) who were at the hotel for a hen weekend. One of the floozies, not realizing I was the wife, let slip that Tom had been in the suite where the ladies had gotten through the piles of cocaine they'd procured. Is it a stretch to assume that Tom was participating in whatever else went along with that? For a New York minute, he saw that he was in too deep and needed me to extricate him, hence the 911 call.

The other influencers were the women he got involved with.

Tom had no powers of reflection and therefore no remorse. When challenged about his behavior, he was unrepentant about—indeed, *proud of*—his unfettered adultery, not merely affairs but also some seriously crazy activity that would make his Swinging Sixties father roll over in his grave: garden variety prostitutes, a stripper, the manager of his luxury gym, sojourns in the rough part of town on weekdays to enjoy whatever could be accomplished in an hour or less, continuous professional development with a pair of lesbian lovers, and, as telegraphed by Tom himself, almost certainly a homosexual fling with a restive young stallion who'd checked Tom out at the luxury gym. He moved onward and upward to full-service escorts and then, apparently, something more unexpected and exotic, something I can barely bring myself to think about. Tom's life was taken over by all manner of sexual activity as well as internet porn featuring stuff I didn't know was possible. Thanks to Tom's growing circle of influencers, hedonism both at home and abroad became his full-time job.

PLOP, PLOP, FIZZ, FIZZ

This incident happened perhaps six months into Tom's avowed three years of adultery. I entertain the possibility that he doesn't remember it now because he didn't remember it at the time. In any event, the incident was probably eclipsed by other extreme activity he was engaged in.

Tom went out on an announced boys' night, which he did two to three times a year. No biggie. I knew I'd need a couple of Alka-Seltzers waiting for him and that I'd have to help him into bed by removing his jacket and shoes. I'd cover him up, let him sleep it off, and give him more Alka-Seltzer the next morning. That was the drill.

When Tom returned home at 1:00 a.m., I could sense he was more aggressive than usual. As with most of us, alcohol made Tom feistier. However, once he reached the falling-down drunk stage, he usually became goofy and giggly and just wanted to have his Alka-Seltzer and tumble into bed. Tom was falling-down drunk all right, and slurring his words, but when I offered him his magic potion, he growled, "Fuck off. Leave me alone."

I was surprised but not yet alarmed. I followed him as he staggered to the bedroom and offered to take off his shoes and jacket for him. Once more: "Fuck off, Nunzia." And then he flopped onto the bed with his shoes and jacket on.

I did fuck off to the living room. Ten minutes later, I crept back into the bedroom, where the bedside lights were still on. Tom was out for the count, so I padded over to turn off his lamp. All of a sudden, Tom—who'd been lying there with eyes closed and snoring like a drunk—bellowed that I didn't need to turn off the lamp for him. *I can fucking do it myself.* How could someone so out of it perceive my presence? And why did it make him so angry?

Tom hadn't finished excoriating me for my temerity in attempting to do exactly as I'd done over the last thirty years. I was a fucking bitch who needed to fuck off. Who did I think I was? He could fucking well go to bed without any help from me. He wasn't drunk, he snarled, and then he yelled again that I needed to just fuck off because I was such a fucking bitch.

Tom was temporarily roused from his stupor and sat bolt upright to deliver a further diatribe at an even higher volume. I was scared rigid by his instantaneous lucidity. He was capable of anything in this state, including jumping off the bed to whack me.

I quickly found myself another room to sleep in and locked the door. When I got up, Tom had already left for work. Usually after such a bender, Tom would still be in bed sleeping it off. When Tom called from work later that day, I was monosyllabic, more angry than scared. Why should I have to put up with the drunkenness, followed by such abuse and terror?

Tom was irritated with my terseness when we spoke on the phone. "Why are you behaving this way, Nunzia?"

I was gobsmacked. "Seriously, Tom, you have no recollection of how you behaved last night?"

He genuinely had no memory of his performance. I recounted it to him in sordid detail, leaving him shocked and regretful. For the first time in more than a decade and a half, I received flowers from Tom.

Over the years, Tom had frequently resorted to calling me a liar when he didn't like what he'd heard, a typical ploy by verbal abusers. On this occasion, though, Tom didn't dare accuse me of lying. He recognized that the night before had been something truly awful, completely unprecedented. He couldn't weasel out of it. I'm certain he thought, *Oh shit. Can't stand the wife, but I really was out of order and can't even remember it. Must have been epically bad.*

I later discovered that Tom had been out with the naughty trader, whom I very strongly suspect of introducing party drugs into the proceedings, which, on top of the alcohol, could have caused Tom to black out, something I'd never known Tom to do. That's not to say, though, that Tom's behavior wasn't a true reflection of his feelings. He couldn't stand the sight of me.

HAVE YOU FUCKING LEFT YET!

When this story takes place, Tom was a good two years into his confessed constant adultery and a couple months into a relationship with a London stripper. We were in Italy for a friend's fiftieth birthday weekend. We left the main event on Saturday night with Tom telling everyone we'd see them for Sunday lunch and wish them a proper goodbye then.

When I came back from a solo hike on Sunday morning, Tom announced he couldn't go to lunch because he had unexpected work to do. After I showered, dressed, and packed, I told Tom I wanted to stay with him out of solidarity. I'd sit on the balcony to read my book and not bother him a bit. I wanted to show Tom I cared, especially because he'd been insisting that I didn't think about him at all. I felt terrible about being a no-show for lunch but thought that demonstrating to my husband that I loved and supported him was more important.

It was all for naught. Tom ordered me to go to the lunch, so I ran downstairs to find a ride. Unfortunately, all the birthday guests had checked out and were on their way to the lunch, a twenty-minute drive away. When I went back to the room to tell Tom of my quandary, he screamed at me to leave and to call a taxi if I needed to. I dashed down to the concierge, who arranged a ride. I then headed back upstairs to say I was leaving, make sure my suitcase was locked, and give Tom a good-luck kiss.

When Tom saw me reappear at the doorway, he exploded. "Have you fucking left yet! Why are you still here!"

I was so hurt and taken aback by this outburst. I just stammered that I was going and fled. Once in the taxi, I burst into tears. Twenty minutes to mull it over left me badly shaken. But the show must go on. I pulled myself together during the drive and was relieved to see that lunch was alfresco so that I could wear sunglasses to conceal my streaked mascara and red eyes.

Almost three hours later, Tom arrived to pick me up from the restaurant. Because we had a plane to catch, we departed pretty ungraciously. However, Tom was no longer ill-tempered, just his usual impatient self. We sped along the autostrada out of necessity and missed the airport exit twice. When we dropped off the rental car, Tom left his new Zegna jacket on the back seat, which I realized only as we were checking in. Of course, I was ordered to go back to the car hire place to retrieve it.

Like I said, pandemonium. I now know the cause. It wasn't work that kept Tom from attending the Sunday lunch. It was Skype sex with his London stripper, who'd been in touch while I was out on my morning hike to let Tom know of an available lunchtime slot.

THE STRIPPER, CONTINUED

On a Monday morning the following spring, after another weekend party in Northern Italy, Tom went to London and put me on a flight directly home.

I'd wanted to go to London too but had to fit in. Tom had made plans and didn't want to hear a peep out of me. Because of his monstrous volatility, I was terrified of the backlash if I even hinted at a change in plan. It's also possible that I subconsciously feared that Tom was up to no good, which would have been another reason to avoid broaching the subject. In any event, I was definitely hoodwinked on this occasion and others by Tom's expertise at bobbing and weaving. He could extemporaneously invent narratives for any tough spot he found himself in.

Even though I hadn't pushed Tom to invent any excuses, he nevertheless came up with a whopper to avoid seeing his own family, including our daughter. Tom called me once he knew I'd arrived home to say, "Please don't tell anyone I'm in London. They'll want to see me, and I really need a relax."

Thanks to the transparency provided by the obligatory three years of financial disclosure during divorce proceedings, I'm now in possession of the facts surrounding the travel plans (and many, many other things). Tom's reason for going to London was to check into an expensive boutique hotel with his London stripper. Their week got off to a sexy start with his-and-her STI tests at a Harley Street clinic. The tryst continued with couple's massages and shopping trips: designer clothes, designer shoes, designer bags, an Apple computer for her, and a PlayStation for the stripper's eldest child's birthday.

Let me tell you a bit about Tom's stripper. You can call her a sex worker if you like, but I prefer not to truck in euphemism. If your name appears on the weekly schedules of two strip clubs, let's just say you're not advancing our cause. If you gyrate on a man's lap wearing only a thong, expecting to be paid for your private performance but calling the bouncer over if the customer gets fresh with you thanks to the hard-on you've just caused, where I grew up you'd be slapped with a label that begins with a C and ends with an E. If you have three children by three different men by the time you're twenty-eight and expect the British taxpayer to heavily subsidize your "lifestyle choices," you're a parasite and something else I'm not allowed to say, lest I offend the readership. If—due to your neglect, irresponsibility, and fun-loving lifestyle—the fathers of two of your children petitioned for and won sole custody, you're a terrible human being who shouldn't even own a dog. Call me old-fashioned.

If you convince my husband to pay off thousands of pounds of your frivolous debts and then send you $100,000 more to finance your new "business," I want to take violin lessons from you. If you then get him to pay for your boob job, you're even more skilled than I thought, and he's even stupider. If you continue to extract money from him, you've managed to entrap him somehow... I'll let my readers come to their own conclusions about you and your sterling character.

I DRAGGED YOU FROM THE GUTTER

Our penultimate trip as a family was unmitigated bedlam. We traveled to the East Coast of the US to visit Dominic, then a college sophomore, for Thanksgiving break. During our ten days in the US, Tom had four major meltdowns and assorted mini shit fits, all of them in front of at least one of our children.

Two of the meltdowns were directed at Dominic, who was reduced to tears at his father's cruelty. It was as though Tom was setting him up to fail with his last-minute, capricious demands and arbitrary deadlines. When the kid inevitably couldn't comply, Tom went mental on him in public. Tom's tirades were loud, abusive, and protracted. During this trip, he even made a New York City taxi driver cry. Tom was *unhinged*. There is no other way to express this.

We arrived at Dominic's campus from JFK early on a Saturday evening and had a pleasant dinner with Dominic, his housemates, and his new girlfriend at our hotel. The agreement was that Dominic would meet us at noon the next day so we could have a quick lunch followed by the traditional Mondo Sunday afternoon hike.

Noon came and went, as did 1:00 p.m. and 2:00 p.m. No Dominic. He wasn't picking up his phone or answering emails or texts. Tom drove over to his house. No Dominic. Tom came back to the hotel with steam coming out of his ears. The other kids and I were worried sick, but Tom didn't care about that. It was all about Tom and his emotions. He wasn't worried. He was angry, fucking angry, with Dominic, who he was sure was just being "his usual casual, careless, inconsiderate self."

Tom decreed that we'd go on a hike without Dominic. Louisa, Jamie, and I reluctantly piled in the car, but Tom was undeterred.

We sped out of the parking lot onto the freeway and then along the rural route leading to the rinky-dink state park Tom had chosen for the hike. When we came upon houses with little kids playing in the front yards, I asked Tom to slow down a bit. What was I thinking?

Predictably, my impulsive request brought about a two-hour-long tirade against me, but I wasn't prepared for its ferocity or insanity. "How dare you comment on my driving when you can barely drive yourself? All those people who comment on my driving...I can drive better than them with my eyes closed!"

I only had the chance to agree that Tom was very skilled.

Tom was soon in a complete state. He was screaming, swearing, and insulting me and all my attributes. His shoulders were rising and falling. His lips were pursing and unpursing. He was frothing at the mouth. His arms became like steel rods jerking the steering wheel. His whole body was in spasm. Louisa and Jamie were as shocked and traumatized as I and knew not to utter a word. My fight-or-flight reaction was that I needed to teleport the three of us to somewhere safe. Honestly, "Beam me up, Scotty" was my immediate emotional response to a surreal scene I couldn't physically escape. I was also still desperately worried about Dominic's whereabouts.

It got worse. Tom's meltdown lasted the rest of the way and the time it took us to park. Other visitors could hear him with the windows closed. His meltdown continued as we walked around the miserable pond and continued until he burned himself out.

Tom had many horrible things to send my way, but the most shocking was this: "I dragged you from the gutter. I pay for your luxury lifestyle. Without me, you'd have nothing, you stupid bitch. If I hadn't dragged you from the gutter, you'd be living like your sisters." Verbatim. He said this several more times just in case I hadn't understood it the first time.

Even if I'd dared speak, what retort could I have made to the outrageous claim that he'd dragged me from the gutter? This insult was unsurpassed in its ugliness, and if anything, it was the other way around. It was I who'd dragged Tom from the gutter, although it would never have occurred to me to think of the chronology of our lives in this way. It was I who paid for all sorts, including groceries, restaurant meals, textbooks, and even Tom's clothes when we were at business school; I who had the connections that got him his first job; I who arranged to house his chronically insolvent parents; I who paid for his sister's private medical treatment when she couldn't be seen by the UK National Health Service; and I who contributed the entire down payment on our first property. As far as my sisters were concerned, they didn't live like I did, but unlike Tom's family members and his stripper, they were all hardworking taxpayers who earned their own keep and lived a decent middle-class lifestyle.

I left all this unsaid. But why would Tom even utter these words? Where had they come from? When I found out later about the benefits-cheat stripper, whose debts Tom cleared and whose business he financed, I understood that Tom had been berating *her* for his having to sort her and her family out with our joint marital funds. This wasn't the first time Tom had transferred his anger at someone else onto me, but it was, without a doubt, the most extreme instance.

Dominic materialized when we returned to the hotel. He'd pulled an all-nighter to finish a paper and then fallen asleep at his girlfriend's. That was his story, and he was sticking to it. It was irresponsible and thoughtless of him, whatever the truth. But it didn't matter. I was relieved he was OK. Dominic was abjectly sorry to learn what his failure to appear had set in motion, but I reassured him later in private that his father bore the responsibility for his loss of self-control. And if it hadn't been this trigger, there would have been another.

A CUNNING LINGUIST

Shortly after we got back from our fun-filled trip to the East Coast, Louisa learned she'd been accepted into her top choice of college, where she planned on majoring in modern languages.

I was in the room as Tom congratulated her and added, with a guffaw, "You're going to be a cunning linguist!"

Suffice it to say, Louisa was mortified.

I was momentarily speechless but managed to squeak out, "Tom, how could you say that to her?"

Tom followed his guffaw with titters at his own knee-slapper and, of course, an admonition that I needed to lighten up because it was only a joke.

Yes, it was a joke, a tasteless and inappropriate one. Louisa and I walked away in separate directions because we couldn't face each other in our extreme embarrassment.

SHUT UP, YOU'RE NOT BLEEDING

Tom's *complete* inability to control his explosive anger, along with his conviction that he was entitled to express any emotion in any fashion in any situation with impunity, started about the time I was summarily banished from the hotel in Italy so that he could enjoy Skype sex with his London stripper. Tom's craziness intensified from there, spanning the entirety of the next year and percolating into the final months of our marriage.

As mentioned, Tom got pretty riled up about politics and was sure his opinions were unassailable. He brooked no argument and could barely conceal his contempt for people with other points of view. At a dinner party we held that final fall of our marriage, Tom absolutely lost it about the threat to democracy from the resurgence of totalitarian regimes around the world.

Not that any of our guests were fascists or supporters or relatives of strongmen. They were reasonable people simply stating other sides of issues faced by countries they'd come from or spent time in. Tom cut them off, shouted them down, belittled them.

As we were finishing up the champagne and predinner discussions, and about to herd our guests to the table, Tom put his hands on his hips and spat out to all assembled, "You need to listen to me because I know what I'm talking about. I have a degree in politics and economics." Verbatim.

I was horrified, not just because of Tom's pomposity, but also because the principal object of Tom's ire was Ken, who has a PhD in economics and is hired by NGOs and central governments to apply his expertise to a range of real-world problems.

While the other guests and I looked on in amazement, Ken and Julie, his almost as highly educated wife, politely and constructively dealt with Tom's verbal assaults on them for having an opinion that was at odds with his. Their gracious behavior was astonishing. (Dear Reader, I hope you've already picked up on the supreme irony of Tom's attachment to democratic values.)

Tom knew he'd been out of order. He approached Ken and Julie before we sat down to dinner to apologize to them both. Tom even hugged Julie as a conciliatory gesture. Even so, not more than five minutes later, Tom was screaming at Julie again because she had ventured another opinion he didn't like. Worse than that, Julie was able to support her opinion by very specific examples, which drove Tom right over the edge. I saw that the other guests were no longer excited by this spectacle but, rather, alarmed and deeply uncomfortable. To Julie's credit, she held her ground and continued to politely argue her case.

Mercifully, the political discussion changed course, but I recognized that Tom was still seething about the challenges to his superior wisdom. There were no more outbursts from him, though.

After everyone left, I said nothing. Due to years of training, I did my utmost to preempt any reminders of the evening's events. Tom could be provoked so easily, especially in this extremely volatile phase he'd entered.

Invoking my well-honed survival techniques was futile, though, because Tom's deep anger at Ken and Julie's audacity had never left his brain. As my housekeeper, helper, and I were clearing up, Tom held a post–dinner party meltdown. It went on for half an hour and was capped off with the announcement that Ken and Julie were "fucking morons."

Tom suspected I shared their opinions, so I stayed shtum. To my great relief, Tom then stomped off to bed, and there were no further ramifications for me.

Or so I thought at the time. Several weeks later, I had dinner plans with Ken and Julie. They'd been very good friends of ours for two decades. Julie and I had supported each other practically and emotionally during each other's medical travails, and I was especially close to her. Ken, unlike Tom, admired my intellect and had hired me to consult on several high-profile government projects. It was demanding but gratifying work, a realm where I could feel competent and validated and enjoy a sense of collegiality with intimidatingly smart people from all around the world. Even though Julie and Ken were constantly on the move, we maintained our strong friendship and mutual admiration society. *I* wanted to stay friends with them.

A couple days before the planned dinner, I had misgivings. I felt bad about deceiving Tom by saying I'd be with Julie on a girls' night out. I also wanted to repair *our* relationship with these two valued friends. I owed Tom the opportunity to make amends. Therefore, I asked him to join us but requested that he avoid politics. He agreed.

Ken and Julie were gracious and receptive, believing that Tom's dinner party behavior had been a one-off. Tom was all too pleased to come along. He was so amiable, in a puke-inducing way that should have set alarm bells ringing in me. He became even more cloyingly sweet when it turned out that Julie was very knowledgeable in a new line of business Tom was considering. He offered Julie a job right then and there, and the rest of the evening became about Tom's business proposition.

I'd hoped to ask Julie and Ken a quick question about the direction of my business, with a view to scheduling a separate meeting to get their advice. Under the circumstances, I never got the chance. That was my fault, though. I could have briefly interjected.

I was disappointed because I knew Ken and Julie would soon be off for a two-month posting in another part of the world. The window for getting their help was about to close. In any case, I was pleased that the occasion had gone so well and that Tom had kissed and made up with these two. I was used to putting my needs last, so I didn't feel any particular rancor.

When we got in the car to go home, I was in a good mood, and ostensibly so was Tom. I chirped that the dinner had been fun and that I was so glad we got the chance to straighten things out. I then went on to say, "Of course it's my fault, but I'd really wanted to get some advice from them. I'll just have to ask them when they come back from their assignment." After the relief of a pleasant evening, I felt comfortable letting Tom know about this small disappointment, one I clearly blamed on myself. I absolutely consider the possibility that I was being passive-aggressive, or at least came across that way.

Tom immediately lost it, telling me it wasn't his fault and how dare I blame him.

I immediately went into defensive mode, saying, "Yes, Sweetie, you're right. It's not your fault at all. It's mine. I'm sorry I didn't make that clearer. What you and Julie were talking about was far more important. I'm glad she'll be able to help you out."

I couldn't get Tom to calm down. Per usual, he wasn't listening to my retraction. He got angrier and angrier. He screamed, he swore. He drove way over the speed limit up the middle of the road, weaving in and out of other lanes, including the oncoming one. By the time we got to our neighborhood, Tom was in a shaking, spitting, uncontrollable fury. He raced down the curvy, hilly road to our compound. The security guard lifted the barrier just as we were about to crash through it.

For a split second, I knew I was heading over the hillside to my death. No such luck. Right after we passed the barrier, Tom called me a fucking bitch and, without missing a beat, struck me with the back of his free hand. I was stunned by the pain.

When I could talk again, I gasped that I was bleeding.

"Shut up. You're not bleeding," Tom snorted.

Ten seconds later, when we reached our parking space, we saw that blood was cascading from my mouth and nose. It ran down my coat and scarf, pooling and overflowing onto the seat from my cupped hands.

We quickly stole into the lobby, looking around first to see if there was anyone about to witness us. We hopped onto the elevator and rode up to our apartment, with me attempting to spill as little blood as possible. Tom wanted to help clean me up and get settled, but I told him to go downstairs to wipe up any blood I might have trailed behind me. While he was attending to the evidence, I was in the bathroom with my housekeeper, washing away the blood on my face and examining my injuries.

Tom had walloped me on my lower nose and mouth, which must have accounted for all the blood pouring from my gums.

Of Tom's thousands of verbal attacks and dozens of physical ones, most of which would count as serious abuse, this particular incident—years after the fact—haunts me still, eats away at my peace of mind. Why was I stupid enough to say anything that could have been construed as the least bit negative? I'd been with Tom long enough to know that saying anything at all could make him fly off the handle. Had I subconsciously pushed the envelope?

What was my thirty-year role in creating a situation in which only Tom had a claim to emotions and emoting? Could I be blamed at all? Or was I completely to blame? On the few occasions I'd asserted myself against Tom, his response was to put me in my place and then abuse me some more. So I can let myself off the hook on this one. Or can I?

Why did I tolerate a long-term relationship in which I was precluded from expressing anger, opposition, irritation, or even confusion? Why did I allow my body to be the shock absorber for Tom's extreme dysfunction? Despite my subsequent education on insidious, shape-shifting abuse, I still cannot wrap my head around the reality that for thirty years I allowed this man to destroy me, physically and emotionally.

Why didn't I take this assault more seriously? It represented an extreme loss of control that resulted in both physical injury and extreme emotional trauma to me and, more to the point, could have ended in death or severe injury to both of us and others. And why were the cops not at their usual checkpoints to intercept us speeding up the middle of the road? Paralyzed by trauma and fear of more, I asked none of these questions. My default coping mechanism was to avoid reflection altogether.

When I cast my mind back to that evening, I recall that there was only one question I was conscious of posing and then answering for myself, namely whether I should go to the hospital. My mouth had gushed blood, and my nose, jaw, and lips were throbbing. I thought I needed medical attention but didn't want Tom near me, so I considered asking my housekeeper to accompany me to the emergency room. Tom's likely response to this course of action struck fear in my heart.

And I was so very tired, the weariness deep in my body and soul. I wanted to go to sleep and never wake up. I couldn't have faced the trip to the emergency room, the poking and prodding, the questions and pressure from the doctors to involve the police. I'd have to pay dearly for a trip to the hospital and all its consequences. No way around it, I'd have to pay, and so would Tom. The whole family would have to pay. Seeking medical attention would be my own crossing of the Rubicon.[26] I recognized that I'd be forcing myself to take further action, terminal action, and that was something I didn't have the bandwidth for. My modus operandi was avoidance: papering over cracks that were, in actuality, miles-deep crevices, gaping abysses.

---

26 I wish I had gone to the hospital then, and all the times Tom gave me black eyes, some of which I haven't had room to mention in this book. Having the medical records as proof of assault could have made a huge difference to the outcome of my divorce.

Despite the never-ending nightmare I was in, the show had to go on. I didn't cry. I didn't bother asking for ice. Instead, I just instructed my distressed housekeeper to go back to bed. I took some Advil PM and dutifully set the alarm clock. I peeled off my clothes, chucked them on the floor, and crawled under the covers. Then I burrowed into bed, where I disappeared till morning.

When Tom came back from cleaning up the blood, I hadn't yet entered the wonderful oblivion of sleep. He said he was sorry—very, very sorry. Then he started yelling at me again because I'd put him in the position of being in the wrong. If only he hadn't hit me, I would have remained completely at fault. I didn't bother responding. I just turned over, and Tom went away.

Tom never followed up with Julie on the consulting gig. He wasn't prioritizing business at that point.

THE WINTER OF MY LIFE

Tom was on the road for good chunks of the final months of our marriage. When we were together, I trod extremely carefully. I greeted him with an uncertain smile when he came home but obviously avoided the contentious topic of supper, which he invariably requested later.

Because I felt so unnerved in Tom's presence, I'd slip back into the study to do some work or read the news. I freely admit that over the previous year, I'd created my own world to inhabit. It was the only way I could survive. But sometimes Tom would inexplicably demand that I come sit with him. As I sat there, he'd focus on Bloomberg TV, his laptop, calls to his traders, and messaging on his phone. He wouldn't hold my hand as we sat together on the sofa, but on two occasions he pressed his on top of mine as though to trap it.

Tom left the conversation up to me. I couldn't fathom why he expected me to entertain him with my inane chatter or why he wanted me there at all. He was seething, and his hatred of me was palpable. Nothing I said pleased him. When I asked about work, he snapped that he didn't want to talk about the office. When I talked about the kids, he responded with criticism of them and me or with admonishments that I should be on the plane more often to see them. (Now I know why.) When I talked about current events, he informed me that I didn't know what I was talking about and needed to go away and do more research.

One evening, I said to him, "I give up, Tom. What would you like me to talk about?"

He instructed me to talk about my day. When I did, his immediate response was "Nunzia, I'm not interested in your silly projects or stupid colleagues."

While I didn't know this series of put-downs was the final devaluing (right before the final discarding), I did see that I couldn't win for losing. I was vanquished, trampled almost to death, and unlikely to be revived. I retreated into myself. I got to the point where I could barely even speak to my housekeeper, who'd been through thick and thin with me for more than ten years.

NUNZIA, WHY DON'T YOU LEAVE?

At the beginning of that winter, I started intensive sessions with Michelle, a counselor Tom had been seeing on the sly. Louisa had let slip her father's yearlong therapy arrangement, so I asked to go too. Tom demurred, but then his calculating brain saw utility in my attendance. As I started with Michelle, Tom started to phase her out.

My first session with Michelle didn't begin well. I admitted I wasn't perfect and said I'd brought my own neuroses into the marriage. I had issues I needed to deal with.

Michelle said, "Yes, Nunzia, you certainly do." With emphasis on the word "certainly."

I thought to myself, *Hold on, lady, this is the first time you've ever spoken to or even laid eyes on me, yet you've already formed an opinion of me and my dysfunctional psyche.* Even so, I was desperate. I gave Michelle the benefit of the doubt in hopes of getting my marriage and family back on track.

The session proceeded, and apart from her unfortunate opening gambit, I found Michelle objective and insightful. At our third session, after having heard my story along with some of the gory detail, she asked me why I didn't leave Tom. She did this in subsequent sessions too. I later surmised—rightly or wrongly—that this challenge was Michelle's way of urging me to leave. I believe that her growing acquaintance with me and my alternative version of Tom and Nunzia Mondo's relationship journey allowed her to figure out what our Christian counselor Charlene had (rather belatedly) figured out a few years before: *Tom was the problem.* No matter what I succeeded in changing for him, he wasn't going to be satisfied and would find something else to punish me for.

Michelle's probing questions had the effect of dragging my depression and anxiety from the depths into the light of day, causing the terrible, undeniable truth to bubble up and permeate my existence. This is the only way I can describe what occurred. Instead of being galvanized, though, I was immobilized. I was already physically and emotionally ground down, but the gradual understanding that nothing was redeemable rendered me practically nonfunctioning. I could barely sleep, and during the day I was on automatic pilot, performing tasks that didn't require much executive function. Even though I kept my chin up and one foot in front of the other, I was incapable of making any major decisions. I suspect Michelle saw that and was doing her best to help me within the confines of her professional ethics.

It added immensely to my stress that I was often incapable of articulating to Michelle what I felt. How could I be so tongue-tied? I could haltingly relate incidents but couldn't string a sentence together to explain the tumult inside of me. This may have been a manifestation of alexithymia, the condition of *having no words*, which I explained in Chapter 7. Not being able to explain the depth of my misery to the one person I could speak to about it left me wretched. When I left Michelle's office, I felt even more wretched because I was left alone with myself and an even starker view of my desolate future with Tom.

My only joint session with Tom, six weeks after my first session, was "certainly" very illuminating to Michelle. I didn't want the joint session because it would fall in the run-up to a trip Tom and I would be taking together. Specifically, I was afraid the first session of couples counseling would open a can of worms, one that clearly couldn't be resolved in one hour. I didn't want to be alone in a hotel room in a foreign country when Tom decided to continue the discussion and impose answers on his terms. As you'll recall, traveling often brought out the worst in Tom, and at this stage, he was absolutely consumed with hatred for me, an observation I shared only with Michelle.

I explained my qualms about this joint session to both Tom and Michelle beforehand but made clear that I saw the importance of it. I pleaded with Tom, "Could we please have our joint session after this trip, when we'll have the chance for constructive follow-up?" Michelle agreed with me, but Tom was angry at my reluctance and continued to pressure me. To show good faith, and because I wasn't really being given a choice, I consented.

To kick off the joint session, Tom proclaimed how uncooperative and unconstructive I was: *Nunzia didn't even want to come today!*

Michelle didn't speak but allowed me to reiterate what I'd already explained to them both. When Tom repeated his accusation (*See, she just digs her heels in. She never wants to make anything better...*), he made the mistake of gaslighting both me and the counselor.

Michelle piped up. "Tom, I heard what Nunzia said, and so did you. She clearly spelled out her reasons for not wanting to come today, right before your trip. And she's here anyway, isn't she?"

Not much Tom could say to that, except to repeat the general charge that I made no effort.

Michelle did me two more good turns during the joint session. First, she got Tom to promise he wouldn't lose his temper or abuse me during this weekend abroad. This was no guarantee of good behavior, but Tom's agreement was an implicit admission that I did have something to be afraid of. Second, Michelle immediately intervened when Tom gave me unsolicited advice. I could tell from the ensuing exchange that Michelle had already spotted Tom's tendency to impose his superior wisdom on others. Even though I'd been given nonoptional advice from Tom for three decades, it was only recently dawning on me that "advice" was an insidious and backhanded form of abuse. It was cold comfort but nevertheless validating to know that someone else had an inkling of what I went through on an almost daily basis.

THE MIXED MESSAGING INTENSIFIES

After extensive travel in and out of our home base during that final winter, Tom returned at the end of March to stay awhile. He didn't like me any better but was in a buoyant mood. He was sure his lavish "marketing" efforts would result in a hefty number of existing investors following him to his new venture and new investors hopping on the bandwagon. Early the next year, assets under management would exceed several hundred million and explode from there! His fund would outperform all others in its category! Massive performance fees would kick in PDQ!

Tom's ego and profligacy grew with every extra million in fees he expected to amass. In between beratings during those final months, Tom instructed me to make a short list of Mayfair estate agents. I'd soon be on a plane to the UK to find us a pied-à-terre in one of the most expensive neighborhoods in London. (Due to the subsequent abrupt unraveling of our marriage, this junket never took place, and a London property was never purchased.)

Mixed messaging had long been a feature of our relationship, but recent inconsistencies, on top of the instruction to find a several-million-pound property in the W1 postcode, were glaring and about to become more so.

In the preceding six months, Tom had stepped up his abuse, assaulted me, and threatened to throw me out, and even divorce me, yet we took four over-the-top holidays during this time. He lavished me with gifts, including a Piaget watch and other expensive trinkets I hadn't requested. Most bizarre of all, in January we moved into a new apartment, one even more cavernous than the last. Tom told me to spare no expense in redoing it.

I couldn't figure out why he'd chosen this five-bedroom property in the first place, given my uncertain status and the fact that we were almost empty nesters. I was also deeply perturbed by the realization that I was tasked with creating the mere container of a home, one I might well be summarily expelled from anyway. Having said that, this project was a distraction and the closest thing I had to a hobby. Probably foremost in my mind: My ability to put together a beautiful home was the only thing Tom still admired me for, the only thing he trusted me to do without any meddling or criticism from him. Despite my misgivings, I craved an uplifting diversion. In short order, I created an apartment worthy of *Architectural Digest*.

Upon his return in March, Tom informed me that I'd be hosting the inaugural gathering of his company's directors a week later at our new place. The pretense of a dinner hosted by Mrs. Mondo compounded the bewilderment that had been weighing heavily on me.

When the directors descended on us in early April, the apartment was ready and so was I, with a fabulous dinner and a winning smile. For once, there were no predinner dramas with Tom, who carried on as though we were William and Catherine, ensconced in the domestic perfection of Kensington Palace. Tom was loving and solicitous in front of his old colleagues and new friends, even calling me "Darling" several times during the evening.

I recall wanting to cry at several points but remaining in gracious hostess mode. The show must go on. However, I'm not sure I engaged in meaningful conversation with my guests. Invasive thoughts were coming thick and fast, and I felt desperately confused, completely off-kilter. *This is an act*, I thought. But then again, *Poor Tom's been under so much pressure. He actually loves me... No! This is definitely for public consumption... He's so sweet, so attentive... Don't trust him... He just asked for my opinion. He doesn't think I'm an idiot... No, Nunzia, get a grip. It's a performance.* I couldn't trust my judgment and truly didn't know what to think when Tom actually thanked and praised me afterward for a job well done.

Of course, the all-male directors were also very appreciative of the food, wine, and setting and were most gallant in their effusive homage to the hostess.

I now have the full measure of these unctuous jerks. During financial disclosure, I discovered, inter alia, that Tom spent $30,000 of marital funds when the group moved "off-site" for two and a half intensive days. Dear Reader, what do you think the directors were up to that meant the expenditure wouldn't pass muster with the new venture's auditors?

After the departure of the directors, Tom reverted to type. Since his aforementioned "prostate infection" had cleared up, he started coming home late again, and far be it for me to question him or complain. Even when Louisa was home for just five days at the end of April, Tom arrived for supper only on her first evening back. On the remaining evenings of her stay, he neither showed up nor called, leaving me mystified. I could understand him doing this to me, but to the adored daughter he hadn't seen for several months? The second evening, we ate without him, but I contacted him at 11:45 to see if he was OK. He was just fine, "having a massage," and only vaguely sorry he'd forgotten to come home. The other evenings, I let it go. Louisa and I didn't discuss his behavior. I suspect she didn't want to know either.

After Louisa left, the few leisure hours Tom and I spent together were fraught, to say the least. Tom abruptly announced outings—

walking, nine holes, reflexology, dinner—and I was required to snap to. Below, I give you highlights of the final weeks of our marriage.

SPIT IT OUT, YOU STUPID WOMAN!

One evening, Tom decreed we were going out to partake of the first shipment of summer truffles and ordered me to make a booking at his favorite Italian. As soon as I dialed, he started in on me. "Have you succeeded? Have you got a table by the window? Who is the chef this evening? Don't fail to make this reservation."

The receptionist and I were communicating as best we could with Tom barking over me. When she put me on hold briefly to find out the answers to Tom's barrage of questions, his verbal assault continued. "Have you made the reservation yet? Tell them it's me who wants a table. *What* is the problem? Nunzia, you are fucking incompetent. Why can't you make a simple reservation?" *Pick, pick, pick, harass, and harangue.* I was flustered, overwhelmed, and brought to the verge of tears. Dear Reader, can't you see? Tom was setting me up for failure, as he'd done so many times. He wanted to definitively prove to himself and to me that I really was as bad as he said and, in the process, bolster his reason for leaving. He wanted to absolve himself by demonstrating that he'd tried. *Nunzia is a hopeless, anxious wreck of a woman who can't do the simplest of tasks without falling to pieces. It's not fixable.* The final discarding had to be airtight.

Of course, we got Tom's preferred table, obsequious service, and three courses of truffles, shipped in that morning. We washed down each delicacy with a different wine chosen by Tom's good pal, the sommelier. Stitching a smile on my face and walking the conversational tightrope, I tasted nothing.

I was beyond depressed at this point. I was an anxious wreck, often stuttering and struggling to finish sentences. My inability to express myself enraged Tom further. "Spit it out, you stupid woman. Why can't you relax? Why are you constantly getting your knickers in a twist? Fucking calm down. NOW!"

In the final weeks and months, I endured relentless and savage haranguing and baiting, which took a toll far beyond the decades of constant impatience and frequent eruptions I thought my body and soul had finally become inured to. Most mornings, I woke up completely unrested, with a physical pain whose epicenter was literally my heart. *That wasn't just a bad dream. This is my life. I'm still here. He's still here. I'm going to live the remainder of my days as a prisoner of this man.* When Tom pummeled me in person or on the phone, sensations of pain traveled down my arms and into my fingers.

No doubt you are wondering, yet again, why I didn't leave. You won't understand unless you've been there. As Michelle the Counselor appeared to recognize, I was barely functional. I pushed myself through each day. My self-esteem was long gone. I doubted all my perceptions. With good reason, I had zero confidence in my ability to make or carry out decisions. My executive functions had been obliterated. I was, in fact, an incompetent fucking loser.

YOU NEED TO HAVE AN ATTITUDE CHANGE

A few days after our truffle dinner, Tom took me to a bar where "two people can have an intimate chat." Once there, Tom demanded my cell phone to text the naughty trader to instruct him to call my number in case of any significant market developments. Tom's phone had run out of juice.

Fifteen minutes later, a call came in on Tom's supposedly dead phone. He took the call outside, although the bar was quiet enough for others to use their phones inside. After that call, a text then pinged on Tom's dead phone! Curiouser and curiouser. I was genuinely surprised that Tom's phone was still working and couldn't help asking who it was. Tom was irritated and curtly replied that it was just his chief in-house analyst texting.

In the years they'd worked together, this analyst had only ever contacted Tom in case of extreme emergency. When I said I could wait until he called the analyst back, he snapped that he wasn't going to return the call. Tom's response was mystifying, but I obviously didn't insist. (As I was to find out later, Tom's two closest lady friends had the same first three letters in their first names as Tom's analyst! This was a fortunate coincidence for Tom, who thought I might have seen the screen.)

These inconvenient preliminaries out of the way, Tom launched into his prepared speech. He told me I needed to "have an attitude change." I needed to start loving him again. If I didn't achieve this attitude change by Christmas, we'd be getting divorced.

A decision to divorce at Christmas would give us time to tell the kids and make orderly arrangements. It would also fit in with graduations and other important events.

After delivering that part of his speech in a measured, calm, and benevolent fashion, Tom abruptly added, in an agitated and threatening tone, that if I went out and got a lawyer, he'd find a nastier one.

Then Tom proclaimed how lucky I was to have him as a husband. *He didn't have girlfriends like other men did!* This was an oft-repeated boast. In hindsight, I realize that Tom's claim of having "no girlfriends" was a hair-splitting exercise for his own psychological benefit. He couldn't say he wasn't having affairs or fooling around. However, since his relationships were with "sex workers," he could avoid the label of *girlfriends*—despite his personal investment of time, money, and energy in each of them.

I was obviously unaware of these relationships at the time and profoundly confused by this roller-coaster of a one-way conversation. I said nothing and registered no emotion. I listened numbly, neither relieved nor angry. When he was finished, I told him I understood where he was coming from. I told him it wasn't true that I didn't love him; there was a part of me that still loved and cherished him. I could see he didn't love me, though, and was acutely aware that he didn't like me at all. He responded to neither count. I admitted I was deeply depressed and twirled around slowly to offer the final exhibit: the decrepit, worn-out, undesirable Nunzia.

We drove home and sat on the sofa to continue a series we'd been watching on Netflix. Over the ensuing weekend, not another word was uttered between us about divorce. It was as though Tom had never delivered the ultimatum. In fact, we watched more of our series, took a leisurely hike, and went out for supper on Sunday night. It was an uneasy truce but a pleasant weekend without incident. Still, I remained bewildered and off-balance. I didn't dare think about the possibility that we were on our reconciliation journey.

WAKING UP, SMELLING THE COFFEE

I woke up on Monday morning feeling profoundly uneasy. Over the intervening days, I must have processed all the BS Tom had spewed in the bar and registered various signs that had been in front of me all along. While I didn't see clearly that he was insincere about the possibility of reconciliation by Christmas, I recognized I had almost no chance of meeting his expectations by any deadline. (After all, I'd endured decades of failure due to Tom's ever-changing goalposts.) That Monday morning, everything was still on Tom's terms. I hadn't had the push I needed to end the marriage.

After Tom left for work, I sat down at the bay window and surveyed the neighboring forest, which was, for the first time in weeks, streaming with sunlight. I thought about all the major upsets I'd tried to pretend away over the past few years. Not just the uptick in corrosive verbal abuse. Not just the extreme, almost demonic, meltdowns, such as my brutal banishment from the hotel room in Italy, the unhinged diatribe when Tom informed me he'd dragged me from the gutter, or the unprovoked verbal and physical attack in the car. Not just the frequent baiting followed by the inevitable haranguing. Not just the false claim of a phone being out of juice before a bizarre, rehearsed speech about the roadmap to divorce.

It was also the insignificant but peculiar behaviors I'd turned a blind eye to. Placing his cell phone screen-down as it charged. Switching his computer screen constantly. Calling to ask my permission to stay at the hotel gym to have a "treatment" when he'd never bothered asking before. Volunteering that the driver from the country club had accidentally driven him to a house of ill repute. Telling me out of the blue, when he hardly spoke to me at all, that a younger guy had checked him out after his shower at the gym. Explaining that the bar we were going to for our important conversation was a good place for two people to have an intimate chat. And having me rub antibiotic cream on his invisible skin rash, the one that went on for three weeks. I'd truly processed none of this.

Maybe it was the coffee; maybe it was divine intervention. Finally, on that glorious Monday morning, I did see the forest for the trees. Tom had been conducting a protracted campaign: the final discarding.

Then it struck me like a lightning bolt that some evidence of Tom's wrongdoing must be at home. I hurtled to the filing cabinets. The hanging file of American Express statements was gone, and I realized I hadn't seen any mail from Amex for quite some time. The file for Tom's individual UK bank account was also gone. After almost three decades of residing in our joint files in alphabetical order, this stuff had been deliberately removed. I got to work with what was still there.

A quick dip into the Visa statements yielded all sorts of unpleasant knowledge about Tom's movements and activities. He'd paid *frequent* visits to STI clinics at home and abroad. In fact, it's incredible to me that he wasn't frightened enough by the frequency or persistence of these afflictions to curb his activity. And there were dozens of charges at seedy local hotels that were not his usual standard.

I also spotted dozens of small, frequent internet purchases under Tom's name in just the previous six months. Expending very little effort, I discovered that Tom had been viewing a massive amount of porn, going on interactive dating and "education" sites, and ordering erectile dysfunction solutions. I simply called the phone numbers on the statements or Googled the vendors to find the phone numbers. When I got through, I would give customer service the transaction code. Easy peasy, lemon squeezy. This was when I learned about "paywall" sites that purport to hide the nature of underlying transactions.

I hadn't yet formulated an endgame, but these discoveries succeeded in galvanizing me, finally, into action. I figured out Tom must be up to no good just about every single day, and I aimed to find out more. I called private investigators to check out prices and arrange meetings. I photocopied statements as well as Tom's passport and other documents. That evening after Tom got home, I ran downstairs unnoticed and took photos of his car and license plate. I needed to have a package ready for the private investigator I'd be hiring.

On Monday evening, when Tom's phone pinged at its charging station in the bedroom, I quickly turned it over. I saw that it was from a lady, who did me the favor of texting Tom twice more on Tuesday evening while I was in the bedroom alone. The messages weren't visible, but I didn't need to see them. It was one of the ladies who shared the first three letters of her name with Tom's other lady and his analyst. I knew for sure then that Tom was up to no good. Later that evening, I moved into Louisa's room. Tom didn't appear to notice.

On Wednesday evening, Tom made a strange announcement: "Nunzia, I'll be out on Friday evening." He didn't ask me to join him, say who he'd be with, or explain what he'd be doing. No doubt there were many, many times Tom had lied about his plans. But this was the first time in thirty years that Tom simply said he was going out; he didn't go to the trouble of fabricating any details. He didn't realize that I understood his words to be a proclamation of his freedom, and possibly mine. I was almost certain that the lady sending the texts would be Tom's entertainment on Friday night. I needed to get proof, and now that I knew for sure that Tom had something planned, the pressure was on. I hadn't yet met with any of the prospective PIs and had less than forty-eight hours to get my ducks lined up.

Thursday was a write-off: I deemed the one PI I met too pedestrian for his line of work. The other PI wasn't available to meet until the following week.

On Friday afternoon, I met Peter the Private Eye, who'd just returned from solving an industrial espionage case abroad. Tom's assignation was going to take place in three to four hours' time. Maybe it was divine intervention yet again, but I knew right away Peter was my man. He took the package I'd assembled and accepted the little money I was carrying as a deposit. Thanks to all the info gleaned from the credit card statements, I was able to direct Peter to the neighborhood where Tom and his lady were likely to end up.

BUSTED!

Peter's team got going right away. These guys were experienced and well-connected to law enforcement. They were stationed on the main artery into town as well as in the targeted neighborhood. Within two and a half hours of saying goodbye to Peter that Friday afternoon, he texted me to say that Tom's car had been spotted driving into town from the airport. Fifteen minutes later, Tom's car arrived at one of the hotels we'd short-listed for the tryst. According to Peter, Tom's extreme speed alerted the cops, who, in turn, alerted the PIs to his route. The PIs took photograph after photograph of Tom and his companion that evening, including from the very next table at the restaurant they had supper in.

AN UNEXPECTED FETISH?

In fact, Peter and crew got a very good look at Tom's lady, who they concurred wasn't actually a lady, at least not originally. Based on Peter's intelligence, there is a high probability that Tom's lady was a "shemale" prostitute. (For the uninitiated, which I was at the time, "shemale" prostitutes are trans women who openly advertise their sexual services as such: top surgery and all the manners and trappings of women, but with their male genitalia left intact. Not being transphobic here, people. "Shemale" is how many of them proudly and graphically announce themselves to the straight cis male market.) From Peter's photos and videos, I judged her to be a good-looking woman with very broad shoulders, a masculine jaw, and square hips. But who knows what she was? I never saw her up close and personal, so to speak.

The next morning, when Peter had gathered enough evidence and had a break from surveillance, he called me to drop this bomb. He asked if there was someone with me because he was worried about what I might do when I heard what he had to say and saw the photos he was about to send. I was alone at a friend's place and told him to get on with it. I was rendered speechless on the phone, but when Peter hung up, I curled up on the sofa, viewed the photos, and sobbed until I could sob no more. I then sat bolt upright, remaining catatonic for a couple of hours until my friend returned to comfort me with her love and a large, stiff drink.

Peter reported that Tom wasn't remotely discreet. Indeed, Tom's brazenness is apparent in stills and video footage. Unfortunately, the nightlife area where Tom spent the weekend attracted kids in their teens and twenties. When at home, our own kids would often head off to this district for nights out with friends. How many of their mates saw Mr. Mondo and his companion blithely exploring the neighborhood hand in hand? Why did Tom not care enough about his children to make the effort to be less conspicuous?

THE PUSH I NEEDED

I was beyond distraught by my discoveries over the last several days, those I'd made on my own and the far more terrible ones Peter had procured for me. I had to keep my wits about me, though, because I knew that my imminent separation and divorce wouldn't be easy. I'd have to make calm, firm, no-taking-of-prisoners decisions. I could fall apart later. On the Saturday afternoon, Peter kept me updated by text about Tom's movements. When it was clear that Tom was well ensconced in his hotel suite, I headed back home to pack and organize myself and prepare for at least one more encounter with him.

Tom hadn't told me he'd be out on Saturday night, too, so I played along. In my texts to him, I feigned belief that he was at the golf club for the afternoon and messaged to ask what he wanted for supper. My texts went unanswered, so I plucked up the courage to call. He told me tersely that he'd informed me he'd be out (he definitely hadn't) and didn't need supper. He then hung up on me.

He got home at 6:45 on Sunday morning. As I heard him stumble in, I opened Louisa's bedroom door a crack to cry out that I'd been so worried about him.

Tom was clearly drunk, probably high, and very aggressive. I was at least safe and sound inside Louisa's room.

"Since when do you worry about me, Nunzia?" came his nasty, slurred retort.

I told him I always worried about him. At this juncture, though, I was past caring, so I didn't put up a vigorous defense. I was toying with him, asking innocent-sounding questions to see what else I could glean about Saturday's escapades. I didn't get much, save for a few flimsy lies. After a few minutes of rowing, Tom stomped into our bedroom and locked the door. As if I were going to follow him in.

I waited until Tom left at lunchtime before leaving myself. Peter's team continued following Tom and his lady, getting more footage of them shopping, including at my favorite department store: kissing on the escalator, buying La Perla lingerie, and going to the ATM. Tom was so out of control and head-over-heels with this lady of his that he didn't care if I or any of our friends ran into him. Peter reported that Tom drove her to the airport in the afternoon.

Peter's first weekend working for me was a resounding success, auguring well for the fruitful investigations that followed.

I didn't go home on Sunday night.

When I didn't return home by Monday evening, Tom twigged that he had a serious problem. Because he came home on the Friday night after his announced but undisclosed activity and was completely unaware of what I knew, he believed I'd come to the conclusion that he'd had a "one-night stand" on Saturday. Little did he know that I knew about the whole sordid weekend and had irrefutable evidence.

The next day, Tuesday, Tom made phone calls to my two best friends to ask if they knew where I was. They didn't. He confessed to each of them that he'd *had a one-night stand that Nunzia must have found out about*, and he was afraid I was going to divorce him. He told them I *needed to reconsider and could they please help.* Each friend reported the same exact spiel from Tom.

Tom was in a total dither. He didn't know what my absence signified. Had I run far, far away? Was I in danger? Or was I at the end of my very, very long fuse and about to eighty-six him? While Tom was worried about all the possibilities, I'm pretty sure he strongly suspected that it was the last one, and no part of him was ready for the psychological or financial ramifications of being preempted by an angry wife demanding divorce. The BPD creep who'd planned on abandoning me was shit-scared of being abandoned. And the narcissistic shyster who'd wanted divorce at some later date, chosen and orchestrated by him, hadn't had the chance to fully "impoverish" himself. Tom was about to get a hint of what I had in mind.

On Wednesday, I went home in the middle of the day to get

some things I needed. There was no reason for Tom to come home at that time, but I had a friend with me for protection, just in case. She stood guard at the doorway as I went into each room to quickly gather up what I needed. Surprise, surprise. Tom walked through the front door and down the hallway. When he saw me in the study, a high-pitched "Hi, Sweetheart" warbled from his throat and then he went to kiss my friend, who was closer to him. She immediately recoiled, and I told him to please go away. I assume that's when Tom figured out that I was no longer well disposed toward him and that I was going to be an intransigent and implacable adversary. He told me to fuck off, went into the bedroom, and slammed the door loudly.

On Thursday, I engaged a divorce lawyer and sent Tom a selection of the PI photos along with a letter requesting that he leave the marital home. Outrage at being busted and my temerity in asking him to leave quickly eclipsed Tom's fear of abandonment. According to our housekeeper and driver, Tom didn't appear remotely embarrassed when he saw the photos. Instead, he was irate, wondering who'd put me up to this. He couldn't conceive that his incompetent fucking loser of a wife had arranged successful surveillance all on her lonesome.

On Friday, he received my divorce petition.

YOU DONE ME WRONG

Tom was the wronged party; consequently, his unreasonableness grew by the day. After a week with the most famous divorce lawyer in town, Tom fired him. Rumor has it that this gentleman, whose commercial colleagues had served Tom for years, had the gall to break it to him that in our jurisdiction the adulterer is required to leave the marital home, not the wife of almost thirty years. Tom left for a second law firm, where he was apparently told the same thing. In the face of rules and facts they don't like, cluster B peeps pushed to the brink will lie, cheat, steal, refuse, deny, and defy.

Accordingly, Tom remained unmoved, literally and figuratively. My lawyer then wrote a stern letter to Tom's new law firm, informing them that an application for an emergency injunction would be filed the next morning. I'd win, and not only would Tom be forced to leave the apartment, but he'd also have to pay my legal costs. Tom's side knew this was not an idle threat and persuaded him to leave. However, in his email informing me that he was moving out, Tom claimed that his lawyer told him he wasn't required to leave; he was leaving out of decency toward me... *Yeah, right.*

I didn't care enough about Tom's BS to write back to debunk it; plus, I knew that any response from me would antagonize him further. My prudence didn't matter, though, because Tom wasn't the sort of guy to go down without a fight. True to his vindictive spirit, he canceled the apartment lease behind my back, leaving me with only two months to stay in my home and no legal agreement for what the kids or I would do next. My savvy lawyer spotted not only this sly, underhanded amendment to the lease but also the fact that Tom had *previously* changed the lease so that I'd have only one month left in my home. (I can only surmise that Tom's lawyers also told him that a judge would never accept that I'd be given just a month to divide up a household built over thirty years, so Tom generously arranged for one more.) My lawyer challenged the two months in court and won, and the judge gave me a further six months in the apartment. Tom was driven further round the bend when he discovered that his ruse had been uncovered and foiled.

Indeed, this dastardly legal measure on my part made me a marked woman earlier than I'd anticipated. Having already emptied the joint household account and canceled my credit cards, Tom was going to make my existence as miserable as possible. Because of the long reach of the US Internal Revenue Service, no assets were in my name, and Tom wasn't going to give me anything at all until forced to do so. He was going to do everything possible to delay and minimize maintenance and the property settlement. Unfortunately, my nominal salary from my company wouldn't cover the enormous household bills or personal expenses. And Tom, as the other owner and director, was never going to sign off on an increase in my salary or a loan from the company. Long story short: two weeks after I left Tom for good, I had $15,000 in cash to my name and was forced to borrow small and large amounts from generous friends to pay for utilities, staff salaries, groceries, doctor's visits, other essentials, and my legal bills.

Tom wasn't remotely embarrassed that friends were having to take care of his wife. On the contrary, he was on a rampage and happy to tell all and sundry that I was a vindictive, money-hungry cow and all-round terrible human being who needed to suffer these privations. Nobody should be helping me out. Be warned, some variation on this theme is likely to happen to you if you divorce a cluster B personality.

After six weeks, Tom fired the second law firm because he decided he didn't like the mediation agreement they'd helped negotiate. Indeed, Tom had reconsidered his position and become so disgruntled that he also refused to sign the formal court order based on the mediation agreement, leading to unnecessary court proceedings and costs—as well as more bald-faced lying that didn't go unnoticed by the judge.

LOST WITHOUT YOUR LOVE

Three months into divorce proceedings, after all the horrific stunts to inflict maximum damage on me, spreading lies about me around the world, and attempting to alienate our children from me, Tom sent me a dozen orchids with a card that read, "Lost without your love…" As soon as I read this beautiful tribute, I ran out of the apartment to grab the delivery man so that he could bring the basket back to the florist.

Apparently, when Tom learned that I'd rejected this gesture of reconciliation, he lay down and wept like a baby. When he recovered from the shock of my rejection, he quickly and easily returned to the seething hatred of me that lasts to this day. When questioned several months later in court about the orchids and his card's lovey-dovey message, Tom said he was merely being nice on the occasion of our wedding anniversary.

LOOKING BACK

The head-crushing epiphany I got when I sicced private eyes on Tom was the reason I could finally file a divorce petition without any hesitation or self-doubt. The undeniable truth, whacking me in the face and smacking me upside the head, was a liberation. The subsequent raft of discoveries of Tom's abject duplicity and disgusting behavior enabled me to stay the course with complete conviction.

After my massive relief at learning the truth about the untruth, the next stage was anger at myself for having been so stupid and trusting. Nunzia Mondo, a sophisticated and well-educated gal with one of the best bullshit detectors on the planet, was legged over by Tom Mondo, the genetically honorable Englishman. The upright guy who'd always repay what he owed you, the golfer who'd never move his ball, the driver who'd have the points taken off his license rather than lie about how fast he'd been going, and, of course, the rugby player who'd never cheat on the rugby pitch.

But also the sort of man who, from the get-go, would cheat on me and lie to me about everything, big and small. Who'd give me crabs and blame it on the hotel linens, gaslight me, and call me a liar. Who'd become so brazen with his deceptions that he confidently fabricated the details of weekends away and got me to unwittingly participate in the phantom skin rash deception against myself.

What matters most, though, is that my liberation began on the Monday morning I snapped out of my torpor, realizing that what I'd just discovered was almost certainly just the tip of the iceberg. I got to work amassing further evidence of Tom's misdeeds and instituted divorce proceedings.

For about two minutes, I was naive enough to believe I'd be able to bring Tom to his knees with my plan of action. Even my unexplained departure from the house was met with an elaborate fabrication to my best friends. That was just for starters. Tom's realization of my inexcusable deviousness—first, having him investigated and, second, serving him with a divorce petition—gave him carte blanche to spread pernicious lies about me in our community and around the world. To this day, Tom besmirches my name to anyone who will listen, informing them that I was a money-grubbing bitch who never loved him.

With a campaign of disinformation and financial manipulation, Tom also attempted to create a rift between me and our children and was partly successful. To screw me in the financial settlement, I believe Tom skated dangerously close to the edge, both in sworn affidavits and through a raft of undocumented "loans" and other dodgy transactions. My lawyers and I also strongly suspect that he committed perjury and fraud. Unfortunately, a subpoena for a person in the know, a colleague who wouldn't have taken the risk of lying in court, wasn't filed in time. Tom's antics also included receiving and sending enormous amounts of money on behalf of others through his personal account, a practice that not only looked an awful lot like money laundering to me but would also typically be avoided by someone in Tom's position. (The judge appeared to take the view that such financial shenanigans were just part of the "rough and tumble" of divorce cases. Accordingly, she didn't allow us to pursue any of these questionable deeds.)

In fact, Tom has no sovereignty over himself and very little self-awareness. Initially, lying was something he did from time to time to smooth the path for the freedom he thought he was entitled to and to get himself out of jams. To my mind, dishonesty evolved into a habit and then became a way of life for Tom.

Through the uneven and difficult exercise of Christian forgiveness, my rage and resentment toward Tom have dissipated. I feel mainly disgust and pity, and only occasionally spurts of anger.

Anyway, how can you rationally feel anger at someone who has the emotional makeup of a four-year-old?

My anger is directed at myself. It was I who allowed this spiteful, fibbing, petulant child to ruin my life. Of course, I'm now educated on the damage BPD sufferers can inflict on others and recognize the difficulty of escaping their clutches. In other words, I know I was, to a great extent, Tom's victim. However, because of my upbringing, individual character, and Boomer status, victimhood is a tough pill for me to swallow. I guess I prefer the burden of my own culpability to the label of victim.

I'm still working through this but doubt I will ever be rid of the profound regret I feel for squandering a life of great promise and causing massive dysfunction to three precious souls.

I'll continue to pray, write, and remind myself that when I got tangled up with Tom Mondo, I understood nothing about spousal abuse, including that the only course of action was to flee—and never return.

You do, though.

CONCLUSION

Dear Reader, you might opine that the saga of Tom's final weekend of in-your-face adultery and clumsy cover-up attempts—complete with snippets from the private investigators' amazing work—and a recounting of the opening salvos in a protracted divorce don't serve the stated purpose of my book. However, it's important for me that you know what pushed me to finally liberate myself from his prison. Tom's lifetime of bad behavior encapsulated itself into one epic blockbuster. I watched the final scenes in living color and figured out it was time to plan and execute my escape.

Our split and its immediate aftermath demonstrate clearly the profound instability governing Tom. First, he wanted to deceive me and figure out in his own time if he truly wanted to divorce me, then he needed me to reconsider my decision to divorce him, then he treated me abominably and fired two divorce lawyers whose legal advice he didn't like, then he hoped for reconciliation, and then he finally and completely turned against me when I rebuffed his anniversary gesture. The final revolutions of the abuse cycle were compressed versions of the cruel and relentless "shifting of sands" I'd experienced over thirty years. Dear

Reader, how my marriage ended is a crucial part of my cautionary tale.

I give you here only a sampling of what I went through in the initial stages of a divorce that took more than three years to complete. (A full recounting would take too long, bore you to bits, and exceed your expectations of awfulness.) My other reason for including the details of the kickoff to my divorce is to highlight the dangers of leaving, even with the most meticulous planning. Splitting up with an abuser, especially one with a cluster B personality disorder, is worse than you could ever imagine. Tom, a financial executive sworn to the highest ethical and legal standards, dissembled and behaved abominably from start to finish and continues to do so now. With hand on heart, my lawyer said he'd seen his share of badly behaved spouses in his day but none quite as malicious and duplicitous as Tom.

Cluster B spouses will create elaborate fabrications to support what they have come to see as the truth. Their damaged psyches cannot allow them to do otherwise. Their alternative realities portray their hated spouses in the worst possible light, and everything else must fit in with their narratives: amended facts, reordered timelines, additional lies, and sins of omission. The more they repeat their stories, the more they believe them. In the often overburdened family courts, these depraved souls are quick to recognize the untrammeled opportunities for lying and cheating with impunity.

I shudder to think what might have happened to me if I had been an unmarried partner in a jurisdiction without common law or other legal arrangements for the dissolution of domestic partnerships. Instead of being merely shafted, I would have been royally screwed. Tom would have made sure of it.

In fact, Tom almost got away with royally screwing me. In the amicable divorce Tom had plotted, he'd have been in the driver's seat. He'd have maintained the façade of reasonableness and fairness because he wanted me to accept 50 percent of the assets *as he presented them.* In his plan A, I'd have been too dispirited and docile to challenge him.

Most important, I would have been unaware of Tom's financial shenanigans. In addition to the extravagant family expenditures I already knew about, he'd squandered tremendous wealth through wildly over-the-top business travel and entertainment, partying, and absurdly generous gifts to his various liaisons. I suspect he also concealed assets by sending money abroad, money laundering, and other financial subterfuge. Thanks to my just-in-time realization that Tom was up to no good, some of his ruses, such as the dozen undocumented loans he made, were thwarted, and his plan A fizzled.

I beat Tom to the punch, which unhinged him further and caused this otherwise brilliant man to say and do irrational and downright stupid things. While on the witness stand, for instance, Tom complained that I'd wasted marital funds on PIs despite the obvious fact that busting him not only proved my suspicions correct, but also stanched the exponentially greater dissipation of marital funds well underway. The judge and others in the courtroom cracked up at this ridiculous and hypocritical accusation against me. Tom didn't get the joke. His pathological hatred of me got in the way. Be prepared for this BS. If the abuser is dogged enough, his deceit and malice will almost defeat you.

But it won't defeat you completely or forever. Do you recall that I was so depressed that I had to push myself through each day, suffering in silence and alone? That the dome of Tom's cruelty threatened to imprison me for the rest of my life? That the constant state of bewilderment rendered me almost nonfunctional?

Tom's brazen adultery and systematic deception in the final months of our marriage could have been the cherry on top of all the misery I'd suffered. However, they were the very thing that pushed me out the door, that liberated me. I won't pretend that Tom didn't inflict lasting damage to my self-worth or that the years after leaving were easy. He did, and they weren't. However, I'm now in charge of Nunzia. My physical and mental health have greatly improved. I'm no longer in the 1 percent—far from it—but that's OK because I derive joy from simple pleasures. Simple pleasures such as not rushing through Kensington Gardens in the spring, choosing to associate with people I like, holding political opinions of my own, going to bed when I feel like it, believing in God—and doing all sorts of things I don't need to worry I will be excoriated or smacked for. Freedom from your abuser: I highly recommend it.

※ ※ ※

I'm anticipating the gamut of reactions to this book, including negative ones. *It's boring. It has too much detail. It doesn't have enough detail. It's not true, or it's at least greatly embellished. There's no way these things happened. Maybe Nunzia Mondo has her own personality disorder and has concocted this whole tale. It's not remotely objective. She presents herself as faultless.*

I wasn't faultless. In fact, there was a six-month period ten years before our marriage ended during which I purposely expressed controversial opinions (ones I actually believed in) just to wind Tom up. I was so resentful of never being able to express what I really thought that I asserted myself in immature and unproductive ways. On the first few occasions, this didn't end well for me. Two-hour bollockings while cornered in the bathroom was my consequence.

After a few weeks of dealing with a feisty Nunzia, Tom pursed his lips, swore, and walked away. I was communicating my displeasure in a passive-aggressive way; I failed to deliver a clear and direct message. Unpleasantness in the form of being controversial just for the sake of getting a rise out of someone didn't come naturally to me and wasn't working. It wasn't a very pleasant way to behave either. So all I knew how to do was revert to my agreeable, placating, roll-over-and-play-dead self.

I also confess that I lost my temper and swore at the end of more than a few two-hour bollockings. I reacted twice to Tom's abuse with my own public meltdowns because I felt relatively safe that Tom wouldn't retaliate in the presence of others. I was right. He just raised and dropped his shoulders in a weary way and looked around with a sad puppy dog face to elicit sympathy for having to deal with such an unreasonable wife.

To you Nunzia deniers, I say Tom was incapable of getting the message, no matter how it was given to him. Tom had never loved me; he was incapable of loving me or anyone else. Period. I loved him, though; I loved him till that fateful Monday morning when I woke up and smelled the coffee. I spent our entire relationship trying to meet Tom's expectations in every aspect, all to no avail. It would always be so.

* * *

I'll end my memoir with this small but meaningful anecdote of an encounter that occurred after my liberation. You, dear Reader, will probably find it underwhelming, but it was a moment of tremendous insight for me. And it may well inspire a hard look at the undeniable truth for the abused among you.

When I made an appointment to tell Michelle the Counselor that Tom and I were splitting up, I was pretty sure Tom had already been in touch to preempt me, almost certainly to give her a false version of events. Lo and behold, Tom had told Michelle that he was divorcing me because I was a greedy bitch who didn't love him any longer. Tom hadn't told her that *I'd* filed for divorce or that *I'd* caught him with someone else. In fact, in the ensuing months, I was to find out that Tom had created a completely false narrative about his life and our marriage, not just for Michelle but also for friends, family, and colleagues.

When I recounted to Michelle what I'd discovered courtesy of the PIs, her mouth fell open and she gasped.

"Nunzia, I'm so sorry," she said. "I had no idea."

As our counselor stood there slack-jawed and genuinely distressed, I went on to tell her that Tom's latest dalliance was just one incident. There was a lot more I hadn't yet shared with her. But giving Michelle a play-by-play wasn't my purpose in booking the appointment. Based on all I'd learned and processed in the preceding month, I was certain that Tom hadn't told her the truth about the divorce or anything else. Judging by her reaction, I was right. I wanted her to answer one question: *Why do you think Tom never told you, the counselor he allegedly trusted and confided in, about any of this?*

Michelle's answer was simple: *shame.*

That's where our session ended.

With more time to reflect, Michelle might have added *and with malice aforethought* to her answer. In any case, her ill-considered, spontaneous response to my bombshell was probably already a violation of her professional ethics. Let's keep in mind, though, that she was reacting in the moment as a fellow human being to some shocking news—and that I was also her client. The fact is that, during their many counseling sessions, Tom had arranged for her to unwittingly play a role in the final performance of our marriage, just as Tom had involved me in applying cream to his invisible rash. By going to Michelle, Tom wanted to convince me and the kids—but mainly himself—that he'd done everything he could to save his marriage.

* * *

Here ends my unfortunate tale. I stayed too long to start over in another relationship but left early enough that I can enjoy a couple of decades of freedom.

Just maybe, as a result of my memoir, you or someone you care about will see an abusive relationship for what it is and leave in time to rebuild a wonderful new existence. Please learn from me. Whatever burdens you carry, I wish you all healing, contentment, and peace.

I encourage you to contribute to a discussion on the roots of and solutions to spousal abuse. Even if your purpose is merely to get your abuse story off your chest, please feel free to write in. You can visit my website, www.peabrainworld.com, or email me directly at nunziamondo@peabrainworld.com. I will publish your stories and your thoughts.

I look forward to hearing from you. Let's get this conversation started.

ANNEX

THE NINE TRAITS OF BORDERLINE PERSONALITY DISORDER

As mentioned in my disclaimer, I'm not making a psychiatric diagnosis, nor am I dispensing professional advice of any kind. However, I did have thirty years of experience with Tom, my ex-husband. The final years of my marriage coincided with an explosion of information on a range of mental health conditions, including personality disorders, which enabled me to educate myself on the topic. In my estimation, Tom checked all but one of the nine boxes for the traits, or categories of symptom, of borderline personality disorder (BPD) found on page 663 of the *DSM-5* of the American Psychiatric Association:

1. Frantic efforts to avoid real or imagined abandonment
2. A pattern of unstable and intense interpersonal relationships characterized by alternating between extremes of idealization and devaluation

3. Identity disturbance: markedly and persistently unstable self-image or sense of self
4. Impulsivity in at least two areas that are potentially self-damaging (e.g., spending, sex, substance abuse, reckless driving, binge eating)
5. Recurrent suicidal behavior, gestures, or threats, or self-mutilating behavior
6. Affective instability due to a marked reactivity of mood (e.g., intense episodic dysphoria, irritability, or anxiety usually lasting a few hours and only rarely more than a few days)
7. Chronic feelings of emptiness
8. Inappropriate, intense anger or difficulty controlling anger (e.g., frequent displays of temper, constant anger, recurrent physical fights)
9. Transient, stress-related paranoid ideation or severe dissociative symptoms

Tom did not check number 5, the box for recurrent suicidal or self-harming behavior.

If a person suffers from at least five of the nine traits listed above, they may be diagnosed with BPD. Tom never got a formal diagnosis as far as I know; however, if you've been paying attention as you've read my memoir, you would conclude, based on the traits listed above, that Tom suffers from BPD.

I don't depend entirely on my biased back-of-the-envelope psychiatric assessment or your opinion, though. When I asked one of our counselors if she thought Tom suffered from BPD, her reply was "I don't *think* Tom has BPD, Nunzia. Both you and I are aware of the extent of his problem. I don't have to say any more." Yes, enough said.

www.ingramcontent.com/pod-product-compliance
Lightning Source LLC
Chambersburg PA
CBHW060523080526
44586CB00012B/589